HISTORY IN HIDING

History in Hiding

The Story of Britain's Secret Passages and Hiding-Places

Stewart Ross

ROBERT HALE · LONDON

Photoset in Palatino by
Derek Doyle & Associates, Mold, Clwyd.
Printed in Great Britain by
St Edmundsbury Press, Bury St Edmunds, Suffolk.
and bound by WBC Bookbinders Ltd, Bridgend, Glamorgan.

Contents

For Charlie, with apologies
that there are no references
to cricket

Illustrations

8 ILLUSTRATIONS

All photographs by the author

Acknowledgements

I owe an enormous debt of gratitude to the hundreds of people who have helped me compile this book. I began my researches by sending out over 300 letters to owners and curators of properties more than about two and a half centuries old which are open to the public, asking if they knew of any secret places on the site for which they were responsible. The response was overwhelming. Many individuals are mentioned by name below. I would like to take this opportunity of thanking everyone who replied to my enquiry, particularly those who took the trouble to write saying that they knew of no tunnels or hidey holes on their property. When compiling a book of this nature, knowing where not to waste time is just as valuable as knowing where to look.

All errors of fact and judgement in this book are, of course, entirely my own responsibility. But, in no particular order and with sincere apologies where a name has been misread or omitted, those to whom I owe a particular debt of gratitude include: Paul Foulkes-Halbard of Filching Manor; Commander Saunders Watson of Rockingham Castle; Mrs Callie Saxty of English Heritage at Pendennis Castle; the staff of the Reigate, West Dorset, Nottingham, Guildford, Exeter, Caernarvon, Llanberis, Ayr, Newton Stewart, Stranraer, Bridport, Lyme Regis, Brighton, Cirencester, Rochester and London Tourist Information Offices; Mr Patrick Phillips of Kentwell Hall; Mr Michael Blair of Wardour Castle; Mrs Sheila Macleod of Muncaster Castle; Esme Ballard of Tamworth Castle; Mr Stephen Weeks of Penhow Castle; the curator of Sherborne Old Castle; Mr John Allen of Exeter's Royal

Albert Museum; the custodian of St Andrew's Castle; Bob
and Martha Bee; Catherine Stark of Sheriff Hutton Park;
Mr Philip Wilks of English Heritage's North Region; Mrs
Dorothy Lock of English Heritage at Berwick-upon-
Tweed; Allan MacCormick of Nottingham Castle Museum
and Art Gallery; Mr Peter Hammond of the Royal
Armouries at the Tower of London; Mr Bob Kingham of
English Heritage at Kenilworth Castle; Mrs Moira Moles,
sometime curator of Hedingham Castle; Corin Shrimpton
of Alnwick Castle; Mr Barker of Warwick Castle; the Very
Rev. John Simpson, Dean of Canterbury; Mr John Corner;
Susan Tomkins of Beaulieu Abbey; Sir Hugh Stucley of
Affeton Castle; Mr John Hardacre, curator of Winchester
Cathedral; Lord Leigh of Stoneleigh Abbey; Gwenneth
Casey of the Priory, Lavenham; Mrs Sally Twiss at the
Devon Office of the National Trust; E.A.J. Cartwright-
Hignett of Iford Manor; J.D. Money of the Leeds Castle
Foundation; M. Roper of Forde Abbey; Mr Ken King of
Avebury Manor (who took the immense trouble of
sending me a hand-written letter five pages long); Gerald
Charrington of Layer Marney Tower; Mr Malcolm Corney
of the Bull House; Mr Edward Hulse of Braemore House;
the Rev. P. Bishett of Doddington Hall; Mrs Doris Sales,
custodian of Hellen's, Much Marcle; Carole Kenwright of
Ightam Mote (though she did her best to put me off the
scent!); Hilary Smith of Wingfield College; Mr Ralph
Vivian-Neal of Poundisford Park; Captain E.H. Lee, DSC,
of the Lord Leycester Hospital; R.J. Charleston of
Whittington Court; Lady William-Powlett of Cadhay; Mr
Mick Scott of the Local History Library, Bexley; S.W.
Davies of Oakwell Hall Country Park; Mary Schofield of
Godolphin House; V.C. James of Kitley; Mr Michael
Hodgetts of Harvington Hall; Mr Brian Carter of
Oxborough Hall; the curator of Towneley Hall; N.L. Lond
of Samlesbury Hall; John and Sandra Bruce of Chingle
Hall; R. Hasell-McCosh of Dalemain; G.F. Hastings of
Rainthorpe Hall; the administrator of Hoghton Tower;
B.T. Ambrose of Cavendish Manor; Mr Robert Parsons of
Newark Park; Viscount Brentford of Newick Park; Mrs
Giles Marking of Toller Whelme Manor; R.J. Hough of

Dunster Castle; R.J. Orr, Headmaster of Rushton Hall School; Mr Timothy Richards of Gawsworth Hall; Sir Thomas Ingilby, Bt., of Ripley Castle; D.F.A. Nicholson of Ludford House; M.H. Barbour of the Mapledurham Estate; Mr R.F. Hesketh of Meols Hall; Mrs C.S. Reynolds of Leighton Hall; Mrs Mabel Richards; Mrs Fiona Tennick; Mr and Mrs Martin Lloyd; the curator of Traquair House; M.J. Robinson Dowland of Turton Tower; Leslie Retallick of Torre Abbey; Mr Stephen Adams, administrator of Little Moreton Hall; Mr Matthews of the Manor House, Chenies; Professor Hugh Edmondson of Huddington Court; Mrs Marian Buchanan of Coughton Court; the Hon. Mrs George Seymour of Thrumpton Hall; the curator of Moseley Old Hall; the curator and English Heritage staff of Boscobel House; the curator of Malmesbury House; the proprietor of the Queen's Armes, Charmouth; the Old Ship Hotel, Brighton; Lady Ashcombe of Sudeley Castle; D.A.C. Rasch of Heale House; Dr Norma Boxall of Bickleigh Castle; Mr David Lee of Moseley Old Hall; Alison Gordon of Tiverton Castle; Valerie Moore of Kirby Hall; Mrs A. Clutton Brock (and her excellent guide) of Chastleton House; Mr Prideaux-Brune and Mrs H.M. Littler of Prideaux Place; the Ship Hotel, Faversham; Mr Norman Kingham of Rock Villa, New Brighton; David Freeman, keeper of Tredegar House; the curator of Minster Lovell Hall; Kate Atkinson of Lyme Park; Mr E.H. St John-Foti of Welle Manor Hall; J.A. St Aubyn, manager of Athelhampton; R.A. Adam, warden of Castle Menzies; Mrs J.C.H. Dunlop of Stevenson House; Sarah Levitt, assistant curator with the City of Bristol Museum and Art Gallery (for information on the Red Lodge); Mr Bill Richardson of Southwick Hall; Margaret Warhurst of Norton Priory Museum; the curator of Overbeck's Museum; Jenny Vernon, curator of Gainsborough Old Hall; Mrs Geoffrey Gilbert, administrator of Compton Castle; Mrs Sally Hopkins, estate manager of Littlecote; A.W. Saxton, estate secretary of the Highclere Estate; Miss S.J. Berry of the Somerset County Records Office; the secretary of Welbeck College; the staff of Hampton Court Palace and the Royal Pavilion, Brighton; Mr Martin Ellis of the Birmingham City Council Museums and Art Gallery (for information on Aston Hall); Mr Cameron Monson of Dalkeith Country Park; Mrs C. Bayly of Plas Teg; Gwen Curtois of Cricket St Thomas; the Museum of London; Kim Robbins and Jack Lohman of English Heritage; Mrs J.A. Aylmer of Nunwell House, and James Taylor of the Imperial War Museum's Department of Printed Books.

Further invaluable assistance was provided by the Kent County Libraries at Canterbury, Sturry and Springfield. The photographs owe much to Mrs Anne Coppin and the Hales Pasture Studios, Knutsford, and Oberon Proofreaders of Canterbury performed their usual professional service with skill and speed. I must also thank my literary agent, Frances Kelly, for her splendid support and advice. I also owe a considerable debt to Rachel Wright of Robert Hale Limited, and to friends and family who offered me accommodation in different parts of the country. Most of all, however, my gratitude is due to Lucy for her impeccable editing, and to James, Kate, Alexander and Eleanor for patiently accepting that exasperating maxim, 'Dad is working'.

Introduction

The Very Groundwork Of Romance

There existed, within the old Red Lodge at Woodstock, a
labyrinth, or connected series of subterranean passages ...
Some Norman architect had exerted the utmost of the
complicated art ... in creating secret passages, and
chambers of retreat and concealment.

From *Woodstock*, by Sir Walter Scott

'The secret chamber', wrote Allan Fea in 1901, 'is
unrivalled even by the haunted house for the mystery and
romance surrounding it.' But unlike the haunted house,
he continued,

> in the secret chamber we have something tangible to deal
> with – a subject not only keenly interesting from an
> antiquarian point of view, but one deserving the attention
> of the general reader; for in exploring the gloomy
> hiding-holes, concealed apartments, passages, and stair-
> cases in our old halls and manor houses we probe, as it
> were, the very groundwork of romance.

An examination of history in hiding, therefore, brings
together a rich blend of fact and fiction. One purpose of
this book is to distinguish between the two. Nevertheless,
while grounded in truth, it also seeks to acknowledge the
important part played by the imagination in vivid
reconstruction of the past.

No discipline requires closer cooperation between
science and imagination than the study of history. A
simple analogy is the creation of a picture by drawing lines

between dots on a page. The dots are facts, verifiable pieces of specific information which, when linked together, produce an outline picture of the past. This process, however, is in itself incomplete. It produces merely a two-dimensional, black-and-white line drawing. The historian has to finish the canvas by colouring and shading the open spaces to produce a work which accords as closely as possible with concrete evidence. The process is complicated by the fact that the picture is never static. History is concerned with time. At its most basic level it is story, the greatest tale of all. Though its beginings and endings are artificial devices imposed to enable our limited minds to cope with its impossible complexity, the past offers every imaginable feature of a successful novel, from fascinating characters to an intricate plot. Truth can be illuminated either by a snapshot of a single era or, as with this work, by moving film which pursues a theme over the years. Both techniques require literary or physical evidence to stimulate imaginative reconstruction. The thread which runs through the following pages is one of the most exciting in history: concealment. Its inspiration is the existence of countless secret hiding places which we know to have been used by our ancestors.

Man is fascinated by the idea of hiding. As soon as they are able to walk, children take great pleasure in concealing themselves from their parents. The elementary game of hide and seek is popular with every generation; indeed, as we shall see, it developed skills in the young Duke of York which enabled him to escape from his Parliamentarian captors after the Civil War (see Chapter 5).

Generally speaking, adults are just as interested in hiding as children. Every year thousands of tourists flock to Boscobel House to peer into the priest hole which sheltered Charles II, and gaze at the oak tree descended from the one in which the king hid in 1651. Equally popular are the smugglers' caves of Cornwall, and the vast underground complexes at Chislehurst and West Wycombe. London's underground Cabinet War Rooms are one of the capital's most frequently visited tourist sites. When English Heritage opened Hellfire Corner, beneath the chalk cliffs at Dover, they could not cope with the flood of visitors wishing to examine the excavations.

Since classical times popular literature has reflected this preoccupation with the covert. The story of Theseus' battle with the Minotaur in the Cretan labyrinth must have been retold a thousand times. In *Woodstock* Sir Walter Scott incorporates the idea of a hinged picture, which he saw at Lyme Park, and a sliding panel is crucial to the plot of his *Peveril of the Peak*. Who can forget the secret treasure trove in *King Solomon's Mines*, set deep in the heart of an African mountain? And the successful employment of the hidey hole by modern writers, such as Daphne du Maurier in *The King's General*, Anna Seaton in *Green Darkness*, and Mervyn Peake in his wonderful gothic trilogy *Gormenghast*, testifies to our unflagging fascination with clandestine devices.

What is it in our nature which is so drawn to the idea of hiding? Partly it is the attraction of the unknown. For all rational explanation of natural phenomena, the world remains a mysterious place and we wish it to remain so. We like secrets, and are attracted and thrilled by the unexpected – anyone lifting the false step at the top of Harvington Hall's grand staircase and suddenly noticing the man hidden below will recognize the sensation. Successful concealment also gives power. As he knelt on a hilltop and watched the Redcoats vainly searching for him below, Bonnie Prince Charlie was filled with a sense of his own superiority. Knowledge of a secret entrance to Nottingham Castle gave Edward III the upper hand over the Earl of Mortimer, and Roman Catholic priests who successfully hid from their pursuers during the reign of Elizabeth I gained an intellectual advantage over their enemy. Finally, there are the contradictory sensations of hiding itself: the feeling of total security in an enclosed space, balanced by the panic of claustrophobia and the fear of being caught. Not many visitors can resist a shudder as they gaze into a cramped hide at Chingle Hall and try to imagine what it was like to be shut inside such a tiny space for days on end.

It is not possible to describe in detail the thousands of secret hiding places in the British Isles. Less feasible still would be an attempt to relate the stories surrounding each one – to do so would be virtually to write a complete social and political history of Britain. Those wishing to pursue their researches into a particular topic are directed towards the list of further reading at the end of the book.

This volume, then, is an introduction to hidden history. It is not the first attempt at such a task, but it is the most recent and differs from its predecessors in several important ways. Unlike Granville Squiers' masterly *Secret Hiding Places* (1933), G. Bernard Wood's *Secret Britain* (1968), Jeremy Errand's *Secret Passages and Hiding Places* (1974) and Michael Hodgetts' definitive *Secret Hiding Places* (1989), which is largely concerned with Roman Catholic priest holes, this book deals almost exclusively with sites that are open to the public.

Despite obvious limitations of space, an attempt has been made to put each hiding place in its historical context, enabling it to be viewed not merely as a phenomenon but as a tangible piece of historical evidence. For this reason the chapters are set out in roughly chronological order. (Those wishing to make a tour of the hiding places in a particular vicinity may find the gazetteer at the end of the book a convenient starting point.) The sites are not simply listed and described in detail, for history is primarily concerned with people, not inanimate objects. With this in mind, much of the book is taken up with stories about the hiding places and those who used them. Only one aspect of the subject of hiding lies largely beyond the scope of the book: though not everyone who wished to escape captivity, hide goods or make a clandestine liaison found a convenient man-made hide or tunnel to hand, lack of space has precluded all but a passing reference to the innumerable hiding places provided by nature.

If nothing else, however, it is hoped that the book will enable tourists, both actual and armchair, to appreciate more fully the vast array of evidence on every hand which links us directly to our past. In contrast to a whole building or a landscape, a hiding place is a specific feature relating to an actual historical event. Though we may read

all the books in the world about the flight of the Bonnie
Prince after Culloden, or the eccentricities of the Hell-Fire
Club, it is difficult to match the evocative power of a visit
to the places where these adventures occurred. This
volume may help the reader to know where to start.

1 Passages, Ports and Mines

But yet I know another waye by an alley that stretcheth
oute of the ward under the earthe into the castell ...
                    Constable Eland of Nottingham Castle, 1330

The ancient city of Nottingham stands upon a broad
plinth of soft sandstone. The rock lends itself to tunnelling
and, not surprisingly, beneath the city's streets there
stretches a honeycomb of passages, shelters, holes and
caves, some occurring naturally, others dug by the citizens
at different times in their settlement's long, eventful
history.

As late as the seventeenth century the poorer people of
the borough were using these burrows as houses, one
visitor poetically reporting that they lived 'like moles ...
earthed in holes' (from Deering's *History of Nottingham*).
This troglodytic habit led a local MP with a social
conscience to speak strongly in favour of Sunday sports as
a way of encouraging his constituents to venture from
their dark lairs at least once a week to partake of sunshine
and fresh air. Some idea of their gloomy existence can be
gathered from the Trip to Jerusalem Inn, the back rooms of
which have been carved from the living rock of the mound
upon which Nottingham Castle has stood since the time of
William the Conqueror. Canny citizens were not above
making money from their hidden assets. It is said that
during the troubled reign of Charles I one Thomas Smith
let out the caves beneath his shop in Peck Lane for the
storage of valuables. The idea proved popular and led to

the foundation of Smith's bank, later absorbed by the National Provincial Bank, from whence it found its way into the all-embracing arms of the mighty Nat West. On a more lowly scale, but still displaying the same native ingenuity, were the activities of Old Rouse, who guided tourists through the complex of caves beneath Mansfield Road. He asked sixpence for admission. Having led his charges down a bewildering path into the bowels of the earth, he demanded a further shilling to guide them back to the surface again. The City Museum is an excellent source of information on the subterranean history of Nottingham, and it is here that the visitor is introduced to one of the most dramatic *coups* in British medieval history.

The scene was Nottingham Castle, the date 20 October 1330. Inside the fortress were Queen Isabella, consort of the recently slain Edward II, and her lover Edward Mortimer, Earl of March. Following the cruel murder of King Edward three years previously the couple had dominated the realm, exercising a cynical tutelage over the young Edward III by taking into their own hands as many kingly functions as they could. The king and his followers were now encamped in the town, where they had assembled for a meeting of the great council. There was considerable tension between the two parties, and eventually the eighteen-year-old king was persuaded to strike before his mother and her paramour devised a way of removing him and placing Mortimer on the throne.

The key to the operation was Sir William Montague, a young yeoman of the household. He approached the king with the suggestion that the man who could best help them was the constable of the castle, William Eland. The story is now taken up by Charles Deering, whose delightful *History of Nottingham* (1751) cites an account of events put together by a chronicler some eighty years after their occurrence:

' "Now certainly,' quoth kyng Edward, 'I love you full well, and therfor I counsel you that ye go unto the saide constable, and commaunde him in my name that he be your frende and your helper for to take Mortimer ..." '
Montague duly did as his master bade him and arranged a

clandestine meeting with Constable Eland. But the news
was not promising. 'The yats [gates] of the castell', said
Eland, 'be locked with locks, and queen Isabell sends
hither by night for the keys thereof, and they be laide
under the chamfell [pillow] of her bed head unto the
morrow ...' Clearly the queen was trusting no one at this
crucial juncture. Nevertheless, Eland had a plan: 'I know
another waye by an alley that stretcheth oute of the ward
under the earthe into the castell.' The presence of the
tunnel was unknown to those in the castle, and Eland
promised to lead the king and his party into the heart of
their enemy's stronghold in total secrecy.

The royal band of eight hand-picked knights and a
number of trusted soldiers made their way stealthily up
the passage from the brewery yard beyond the castle
walls. Once inside they made straight for the queen's
chamber, where they were certain of finding their
principal quarry. The sound of their clattering roused
some of the guards, two of whom were killed in the
ensuing scuffle. Within seconds, however, the assault
party had reached its destination. Edward's men flung
open the doors of the state apartments, seized Mortimer
and, with the queen's entreaties ringing in their ears,
hauled him off down the way they had entered. The
avaricious baron was taken to London and executed at
Tyburn a month later.

'Mortimer's Hole' was rediscovered in 1864. Though it
may not be the exact passage used by King Edward and
his raiding party, it is open to the public and visitors can
now explore the heart of the rock which witnessed such
dramatic events more than six and a half centuries ago.

The other medieval British castle with famous underground works is Dover, the 'key to England'. Here too the
underlying rock is soft and ideal for tunnelling, though it
is not limestone but the celebrated white chalk, which
gives the nearby cliffs their distinctive hue. The first
excavations at Dover came about as a result of a long siege
during the time of King John (1199–1216).

It is well known that towards the end of his reign John
was faced with a massive baronial revolt that led to his

signing the Magna Carta. Since they planned to remove
John from the throne, the rebels needed a suitable
replacement. Their choice was Prince Louis of France,
who had a reasonable claim to the English throne.
Landing in England early in 1216 to seize his unexpected
inheritance, Louis promptly laid siege to Dover Castle.
The citadel's weakest point was its northern flank, where
John had constructed a daunting outer gate, and it was
here that the intended usurper concentrated his attacks
against the garrison of the loyal Hubert de Burgh. Where
the ground was suitable for such tactics, before the
invention of gunpowder the most effective way of
breaching the walls of a castle was by mining. (This,
incidentally, is why the rock-based castles of Scotland
generally proved so formidable.) Louis' men seized the
outwork defending the gate then proceeded to burrow
away beneath the east tower of the gatehouse. When the
structure had been completely undermined, they set fire
to the wooden props supporting the roof of their tunnel,
bringing the whole edifice above it crashing to the ground.
There followed desperate hand-to-hand fighting in which
the defenders managed to seal the gap in their defences
with a temporary wooden wall. This held out until the
death of King John, the accession of the uncontroversial
infant Henry III, and the eventual withdrawal of Louis and
his besieging army.

The lessons of this siege were not lost on those
rebuilding the castle at the cost of some £7,500 over the
next forty years. The northern gatehouse was closed with
a broad complex of lofty towers, subsequently lowered in
Napoleonic times to accommodate artillery. Before this
bastion a new tower (named somewhat incongruously
after St John) was raised overlooking the spur from which
the dangerous assault of 1216 had been launched. The
spur itself was heightened, although its exact nature is
difficult to envisage owing to later alterations. Most
interesting of all, however, was the excavation of a long
tunnel linking the castle with the St John's tower and the
spur, enabling men to be brought forward in complete
safety when an attack was threatened from that quarter.

Though it has been extensively modified over the years, visitors can still venture down this gloomy passage and wonder at the formidable array of thirteenth- and nineteenth-century portcullises, booby-traps, doors and hidey holes which ensured that, unlike Mortimer's Hole at Nottingham, this tunnel was never to be a safe entry into the castle above.

The early thirteenth-century improvements carried out at Dover also included the construction of a sally port, known as the Fitzwilliam Gate, to the north-east of the vulnerable spur. A sally port, sometimes known as a postern gate, was simply a small and easily defended doorway through which defenders could both make an unexpected counter-attack on their assailants and take in supplies when under siege. Almost all major castles were equipped with such a device, though some were better concealed than others. That at Dover was of the more obvious variety, leading over the defensive ditch by a covered causeway to the bank on the far side. The sally ports of the Percy stronghold at Warkworth (Northumberland) and Castle Hedingham (Essex) led directly into storerooms, so presumably they were intended more for the clandestine topping up of provisions than for launching surprise attacks upon besiegers. Unfortunately the passage at Hedingham caved in long ago and was completely filled in 1981; its entrance can still be seen in the south-west corner of the basement storage area.

The sally port at Scarborough Castle in North Yorkshire can be seen at the southern tip of the curtain wall, near where Charles's Tower once stood. The door originally gave access to a steep path leading down to the harbour, protected on its western flank by a stone wall. In later years the steps were used to approach the South Steel Battery on the shore, which was last rebuilt at the time of the 1745 Jacobite rebellion. Like that at Scarborough, the postern gate in Rosamund's Tower at Pickering Castle (also in North Yorkshire) was plainly visible to attackers. It had its own drawbridge over which rapid sorties could be made when the building was under siege, while the great depth of the moat before the entrance ensured that it was not a weak point in the defences. The door to what was once a sally port in the Tower of London is still visible, but, like Hedingham, the passage itself is blocked. One would expect a building with so sinister a reputation as the Tower to be riddled with secret passages and chambers of some sort, but though there are damp dungeons, broad drains and even an underground railway from the basement of the West Tower to a riverside wharf, for reasons of security and safety the monument's thousands of visitors are not permitted or encouraged to explore the building's darker recesses. The only niches which might be regarded as secret are two cubbyholes behind the clock on the Waterloo Barracks. It is said that these were used as punishment cells for wayward soldiers and others detained within the Tower against their wishes.

At Kenilworth Castle in Warwickshire the sally port was enlarged into the Elizabethan Gatehouse in 1570, and there also used to be a small door in Mortimer's Gate when it served as the principal entrance. Alnwick Castle's (Northumberland) sally port also had defences all to itself, known as the Postern Tower. Since 1826 it has housed the Duke of Northumberland's collection of antiquities.

One of the best examples of a truly secret sally port is at Warwick Castle. In fact it is so well hidden that it is easy for the visitor to miss it altogether. The doorway nestles in a sheltered wall of the polygonal Clarence Tower, one of a pair of similar structures flanking the castle's north-western entrance. These are all that remain of a gigantic keep-gatehouse begun by Richard III but never completed. The sally port holds an ingenious position, invisible to anyone walking round the walls from the far side of the ditch, and therefore safe from bombardment. The small doorway is covered by arrow slits and watched over by an impressive machiolated lookout post, known as the Crow's Nest. Moreover, because it is tucked in close to the wall at the rear of the tower, there is insufficient space for assailants to manoeuvre a battering ram before the portal. The only way for hostile forces to effect an entry at this point was to advance to the door and set fire to it, at considerable risk of being hit by covering fire or missiles dropped from the wall head. There is no record of anyone being either intrepid or foolhardy enough to attempt such a venture. The modern visitor is requested to view this most excellently sited sally port from inside the Clarence Tower, and not by clambering up the grassy bank before it. The magnificent castle boasts of no other secret passages or rooms. The covert positioning of the privies hidden behind panelling and tapestry in the Green Drawing Room and the Queen Anne Bedroom is due entirely to social not military discretion.

Berwick-upon-Tweed in Northumberland was once the most contested town in Britain. For centuries it passed like a military shuttlecock between the English and the Scots, and was confirmed as part of England only when James VI acquired the throne of that country in 1603. Even then it found itself separated from the county to which it had given its name – Berwickshire is in Scotland. Though the town's defences were ravaged and rebuilt on several occasions during its turbulent history, we are still left today with one of the finest examples of a fortified town in Europe. There is a sally port near the bridge over the Tweed on the south-western flank of the walls. Nearby several tunnels lead from the quay beneath the fortifications to cellars and gardens within the citadel. Constructed to facilitate the transfer of goods from the riverside to the town, they proved rather a liability when it came to defending that part of the stronghold.

Much of Berwick's existing fortification dates from early in the reign of Elizabeth I (1558–1603) and provides a splendid example of how military engineers tried to come to grips with the problem of defending a site against cannon fire. One of the devices they employed was the bastion, a huge projection in the shape of an arrowhead, which replaced the tower of the medieval castle. The bastions at Berwick stick out from the walls like huge letter Ls. They are attached to the rest of the defences by narrow necks, known as gorges, which run to the walls like arrow shafts from the right angles inside the points of the bastions. This design leaves small spaces, or flankers, within the recesses of the bastions, whose purpose was to provide enfilading fire across the face of the walls. (If all this seems rather complicated to those not versed in the intricacies of military architecture, all becomes clear as soon as visitors see the fortifications themselves. Iain Macivor's comprehensive and scholarly guide book is also a great help.) The reason for our particular interest in the flankers is that they were linked to the town by special access tunnels which enabled men to move safely and secretly into position unobserved by enemy lookouts. Although for security reasons the flankers have to be kept closed to the general public, the custodian is normally able to show them to interested parties.

There are a number of other castles open to the public which contain passages or secret rooms. There are even more which are supposed to possess such hidden delights, though these exist largely in the imagination or the hazy memory of elderly citizens living in the vicinity of the monuments.

Reigate Castle no longer stands, but the ground beneath the Surrey town resembles a piece of archaeological Gruyere cheese almost as much as that below Nottingham. A story tells that there used to be a tavern in the town known as the Three Pigeons, infamous as a den of petty thieves and gamblers. Several times the police raided the place, but on each occasion they found the bar mysteriously empty when they arrived, and they failed to apprehend anyone. The explanation was simple: when a lookout warned of the constables' approach, customers who had something to fear from such a visitation scrambled into the caves and passages beneath the pub. The arm of the law, so vigilant on the surface, was wary of extending itself below ground where goodness knows what fate might have befallen an officer groping around in the network of dark tunnels. In 1923 part of the Three Pigeons collapsed into its own cellars and the rest of the building was pulled down.

The mound on which the castle stood, part of which is bored through by the A217, is riddled with passages. They are known collectively as the Barons' Cave. The name is supposed to originate from a fictional gathering of the rebel barons before the confrontation with King John at Runnymede. There is no historical evidence whatsoever for this, and no explanation is put forward as to why these powerful men, possessed of numerous secure and comfortable castles, should have chosen to meet in a hole in the ground. The most likely reason for the misnomer is that the caves were originally called after someone with a name like Brown, which was subsequently corrupted and a suitably romantic interpretation provided by an amateur antiquarian with a lively imagination. The longest tunnel may well have served as a sally port for the castle, though there are those who claim that the holes were mines dug to extract the fine sand which used to be employed to blot ink and in the manufacture of glass and an unpleasantly coarse soap. The entrance to the Barons' Cave on the summit of the attractive castle mound is clearly marked with a large stone pyramid and on a western slope one of the exits can be seen behind ivy-clad iron railings. At the moment of writing the cavern is closed after an unfortunate spate of vandalism, but it is hoped that the celebrated secret way will be open for public inspection in the near future.

A small tunnel leads from the cellar of Filching Manor in East Sussex, a fascinating late medieval manor house believed to stand on much older foundations. The passage entrance is level with the basement floor and the presence of grooves, cut like a draining board, suggests that at some time in its history the sloping brick-lined shaft served as a drain. But the basement itself is dry and it is unlikely that such an elaborate soakaway would have been built to handle the sewage from the manor's privies. The present owner of the property, Mr Paul Foulkes-Halbard, is sure that the tunnel was first excavated to provide those in the house with a secret means of egress in times of danger, and he believes that it ran a considerable distance to the other side of the small valley lying to the north of the manor. He hopes to have the tunnel on public view in the not too distant future.

There is almost certainly a secret chamber beneath

Kentwell Hall in Suffolk. A record of it was made over forty years ago by the local archaeologist, who also happened to be the village policeman. From the estate carpenter he learned of a sizeable room, with oak boards on the floor, which could be approached down a tunnel about 1 metre high and 200 metres long. Tradition holds that the passage once led to a neighbouring church about 1.5 kilometres distant; in fact, it was almost certainly built as an overflow for the moat. No one has yet come up with a credible explanation for the presence of the hidey hole, and expeditions mounted by the present owner, Mr J. Patrick Phillips, have failed to locate it.

Tunnel seekers may have more joy at Tiverton Castle (Devon), which also has a secret passage. It must be emphasized, however, that entry into this and most other such subterranean ways is neither permitted nor advisable: as recently as the summer of 1989 part of the roof of Tiverton's tunnel caved in and its entrance is blocked by fallen debris. Nevertheless, it is a rare and fine example of a genuine secret passage, and one which may well have been used on at least one occasion. Like most underground ways it was probably first built as a drain, then later adapted for other uses. It has two entrances, one in the garden beneath the bastion and a second, less attractive one at the base of the privy in the Round Tower. There are supposed to be a number of exit points, although no one has explored them recently. Two are in the church and one in the Red Lion hostelry.

In October 1645 Tiverton Castle was besieged by Parliamentarian forces under the command of General Fairfax. After three days' bombardment skilful shooting managed to sever the chains holding up the drawbridge, bringing it crashing down and opening up a direct means of entry for the besiegers. History records that the garrison of 250 men promptly surrendered. Local gossip tells a different story: preferring the stench of drains to the prospect of a term in a Roundhead jail, many Royalists crawled through the sewage of the castle's underground passage (less than 1 metre high) and so escaped into the town. We are not told what sort of reception was afforded the distinctly malodorous refugees when they struggled out of their tunnel, but Parliamentarian bloodhounds can have had little trouble picking up their scent.

Although Sissinghurst Castle (Kent) is better known for the beauty of its gardens than for stories about its drains, like Tiverton it also boasts a celebrated subterranean escape. At the time of the Seven Years War the building was converted into a prison for French sailors taken by the Royal Navy. The historian Edward Gibbon, who later acquired enduring fame for his survey of the *Decline and Fall of the Roman Empire*, did a spell of guard duty there, and was horrified by the 'inconceivable dirtiness' of the conditions in which the unfortunate prisoners were held. At times as many as 3,000 of them were crammed into the converted ruin. The inmates expressed their discontent by smashing up their quarters and being as disruptive as possible: they killed a guard by dropping a bucket on his head from the top of the tower; one group plotted to escape by blowing a hole in the walls with smuggled gunpowder; and one man managed to have part of his sentence remitted by marrying a girl from the village nearby.

The most famous escape, reminiscent of the exploits of British POWs held in Germany during the Second World War, involved a seaman named Artus and a number of his colleagues. They discovered a way out of the castle through an old privy which led to the moat via a drain. One moonlit night, having bribed one of the guards patrolling the castle's extremities, the party set out. The first batch of escapees managed to get over the moat and into the field on the other side, but the second group, including the unfortunate Artus, were seen by a guard whose palm had not previously been greased by French gold. Despite crying out loudly that he surrendered, Artus was viciously stabbed by a bayonet then killed by a point blank shot which blew his head off. A short while later three other prisoners were dragged from their place of concealment in the drain. The passage was subsequently blocked off to prevent its further use as a means of illicit egress, though about sixty years ago an unexplained tunnel some 30 metres long, apparently lined with parts of dismantled fireplaces, was discovered in the castle grounds. As they saunter through Sissinghurst's tranquil gardens, visitors may care to spare a thought for the unhappy Artus and the unpleasant alarums which occurred beneath their feet more than two centuries ago.

There is another tunnel story connected with Sissinghurst, though it is almost certainly untrue. It concerns 'Bloody Baker', a sixteenth-century owner of the castle who enticed girls from nearby Cranbrook into a long underground passage leading from the village to the mansion. The maids who entered the tunnel were never seen again, until one lass managed to escape from Baker's clutches, carrying with her the severed hand of one of her less fortunate predecessors as evidence of the sadistic bluebeard's horrifying exploits.

At least two Scottish castles are supposed to have possessed sally ports. One led from the small postern in the northern wall of the massive medieval stronghold at Kildrummy in Grampian; the other was described in great detail a century ago by MacGibbon and Ross in their magisterial work on the *Castellated and Domestic Architecture of Scotland*. The Goblin Hall was a vaulted structure, furnished with its own fireplace and chimney like a ventilation shaft in a railway tunnel, carved from solid rock beyond the northern wall of Yester Castle (Lothian) and is referred to in Walter Scott's *Marmion*. It branched in two directions towards surrounding burns and was defended with an elaborate complex of doors and portcullises. But sadly the castle is now a total ruin, not even marked on tourist maps.

This is fortunately not the case with Old Wardour Castle in Wiltshire, where two underground passages have been located. One served as a sally port, the other was probably a drain. During the Civil War the besieging Parliamentarian forces of Sir Edward Hungerford detonated a mine in one of the tunnels; the story of the subsequent flight of Lady Arundell through the other passage to Pyt House, 1.6 kilometres away, is certainly aprocryphal. Sally ports have also been located at Windsor Castle (Berkshire):

one runs from the main floor of the Curfew Tower, which is open to the public, to a point about halfway across the street running outside the castle walls; two others lead from the Upper Ward of the castle into the defensive ditch. The Geological Department of Exeter University is currently investigating an interesting tunnel found recently at Bickleigh Castle (Devon).

A number of medieval castles have mysterious or partly hidden passages above the ground. Though these are not strictly secret, they would probably not have been known to besieging forces and could therefore have been used for the clandestine movement of men and equipment. The unusual path cut into the cliff face at Carreg Cennen (Dyfed) is a good example, as is the secret corridor in the thickness of the Peel Tower at Muncaster (Cumbria), which may have been used by King Henry VI after the battle of Hexham. There are two similar intra-mural passageways at Tamworth Castle in Staffordshire. For reasons of safety only one is open to the public.

Wales' oldest lived-in castle at Penhow in Gwent has no secret passage, but it boasts a good example of another secret medieval defensive device: the trick step. The phenomenon at Penhow is located on the stairway leading up to the Seymour Chamber and it consists merely of one tread being an inch higher than the rest. As a result the unwary are liable to stub their toes on the raised stair, causing them to cry out, fall or reveal their presence in some other way. Thus intruders were prevented from making their way stealthily up the stairway and taking the Seymours unawares. Those who are sceptical of the reliability of so simple a device have only to talk to the number of tourists who have fallen prey to it to realize its efficacy. (It should be pointed out that visitors to the castle are warned of the danger in a taped guide, but there are plenty who forget the caveat.)

Rumours of tunnels in medieval castles abound. It is said that Hereford Castle once housed a chapel dedicated to St Guthlac, beneath which a subterranean way led to the river below. Old men have recollected finding its entrance when young, but when asked to return to the spot in later life they are unable to do so. The tunnels leading from the castles at Skipton, Pendennis, Dunster, Arundel, Bodiam, Guildford, Sheriff Hutton and Sherbourne appear equally mythical. Coins are supposed to have been found in the latter, which led to Sherbourne Abbey. However, as the present custodian points out, to make this journey the passage would have to fall at least 20 metres and pass twice beneath the river. The secret passage at Rockingham Castle (Leicestershire), now blocked up, probably provided an escape route into the park nearby. In 1216 King John lost a sizeable portion of his treasure in the marshes of the Wash when the royal baggage train was overtaken by the rising tide. The valuables which he managed to retain are said to lie in an iron chest somewhere in a hidey hole at Rockingham, though no trace of them has ever been located. It is curious how the much-maligned John features so frequently in stories of subterfuge and secrecy.

We have already seen at Dover how effective mining was as a way of breaking down a castle's defences. Unfortunately, very few traces of such work can still be seen. Exeter Castle (Devon), which stood upon rock as easily penetrated as that of Reigate or Nottingham, has been destroyed. The fortress was served by sally ports through which the garrison hampered the siege of King Stephen in the twelfth century, and mines were dug beneath its walls during the Civil War. Sadly, no signs of this military work remain, though the cavity found beneath the city centre's Boots in the 1930s may have been part of a mine. Exeter's splendid array of underground passages, which are open to the public, were constructed to bring water to the city, though it used to be thought that they were constructed for a less public-spirited purpose.

Rochester Castle was undermined by King John (who else?) in 1215. The king had spent the month of September at Dover, recruiting continental mercenaries for his post-Magna Carta campaign against the continuing baronial revolt. Upon taking the road to the rebel headquarters at London in early October, John found the great Medway citadel held against him. He promptly broke down the Rochester bridge, thus cutting off the garrison from relief from London, stormed the town, and settled down to reduce the castle. Before long the royal sappers had succeeded in breaching the outer wall with a mine, traces of which have been located by archaeologists.

The engineers then set about the far more difficult task of bringing down the massive square keep into which the garrison had withdrawn. The siege lasted for about six weeks, and at the end of it the besieged were forced to adopt a diet of horseflesh and water. It was not starvation, however, which eventually led to the castle falling into John's hands, but a skilfully worked mine. The roof of the tunnel dug beneath the south-east corner of the tower was supported on wooden pit props. When the vault had been completed the king commanded that forty fat pigs be brought to Rochester. These were duly slaughtered, their fat spread around the wooden supports and the whole combustible concoction ignited. The effect was remarkable. The mine caved in, bringing with it the whole of the south-eastern angle of the keep. Those of the demoralized garrison who were still fit enough to fight withdrew behind a massive cross-wall, from where they continued their resistance for a while longer. The sick and wounded were expelled from the ruins and trusted to the mercy of King John. Unluckily for them this quality was never one of the king's more pronounced assets, and towards the end of his career it was even more strained than usual: the expellees had their hands and feet amputated. A few days later the remainder of the garrison surrendered. Though the successful mine was destroyed at the moment of its firing, the rebuilt cylindrical corner of Rochester keep endures as a monument to the secret activities carried out in that quarter in the early thirteenth century.

By far the best example of a mine, and one which can be visited in complete safety, is at St Andrews Castle, Fife. The building, the oldest parts of which date back to the early thirteenth century, is unusual in that it was the seat not of a secular magnate but of the bishops and archbishops of St Andrews, for many years the primates of all Scotland. Our story begins in the mid-sixteenth century, at the time of Cardinal Archbishop David Beaton (1494–1546), one of Scotland's last great Catholic prelates. As Chancellor, Beaton led the fiercely anti-English faction who opposed Henry VIII's plan to betroth his son Edward to Mary, the infant Queen of Scots. Henry responded to the Scot's rejection of his plan by sending the Earl of Hertford into Scotland on a campaign of pillage, known as the 'Rough Wooing'. As a result of this the Cardinal undertook to strengthen his castle in 1546; but when the attack came it was not from the quarter which he had anticipated.

Beaton had enemies in Scotland as well as south of the border, for he was a keen upholder of the unreformed religion and a vigorous persecuter of Protestants. He earned their undying hatred by ordering the burning of the popular preacher and scholar George Wishart before St Andrews Castle in 1546. The strengthening of the archepiscopal stronghold gave the Protestants just the opportunity they had been waiting for. A number of them mingled with the workers entering the castle at the start of the day and proceeded to invest the fortress before the garrison fully realized what was going on. The detested archbishop was murdered and his body hung from the battlements. But hardly had the victorious Protestants finished giving thanks to God for their safe delivery from a cruel persecutor than they were confronted by a yet more powerful force.

During Queen Mary's minority the regent and leader of the Catholic pro-French party was Mary of Guise, widow of James V. Before long her government forces, supported later by a French fleet, were besieging St Andrews. Particular damage was wrought by artillery sited on the steeple of the nearby college and at the wall head of the abbey church. The defenders were assisted by Henry VIII, against whom, ironically, the Cardinal had been rein-forcing his castle when it fell to the Protestant *coup*, and despite the ferocious bombardment to which they were subjected they managed to hold out for a full year,

The most interesting part of the siege was the mining undertaken by engineers on both sides. The government forces clearly envisaged a long siege from the outset, for the mine they undertook was a massive affair, over 2 metres high and almost as wide. Pit ponies were used to transport the debris from the rock face and would no doubt also have been employed to carry explosives into the mine if it had been completed. The shaft ran from beneath a recently constructed house in Castle Wynd towards the key point of the fortress, known as the Fore Tower. Miners hewed their way through the rock to a point some 8 metres from the tower, where they broadened the tunnel into a chamber known as a mine head. This was a proposed gathering point for a number of smaller passages which were to extend in several directions beneath the walls, to be filled with gunpowder, then detonated. Had the plan been put into operation, there is little doubt that the castle would have been rendered indefensible almost instantaneously. As it turned out, however, the tunnellers progressed no further than the mine head.

The science of counter-mining was less exact than that which it sought to abrogate. To begin with, it was not always clear to a garrison when their besiegers were resorting to mining, for the works were often carefully shielded from the sight of those on the walls. Secondly, once it was clear that mining was in operation, the garrison had the greatest difficulty in ascertaining exactly where the tunnel was being driven. This was a quandary which clearly exercised the minds of those responsible for defending St Andrews, for they dug two reconnaissance pits before sinking their main shaft, and even this makes a false turn to the left for a few metres before striking out towards the mine head of the attackers. The accepted method of working out whether a mine was being dug was to place on the ground vessels filled with water. Rippling on the surface of the liquid indicated the likelihood of mining in the vicinity.

There was also controversy among counter-miners on how to approach an enemy tunnel. Some preferred to pierce hostile workings from above, thus enabling the defenders to shoot down upon the workmen beneath them. Others advocated digging below a mine, then either blowing it up or smoking out the miners. At St Andrews the former tactic was employed, and supple visitors can enjoy the experience of clambering through the opening pierced between the mine and the counter-mine. There is no other comparable site in the British Isles.

Though the successful counter-mining saved the walls of St Andrews Castle from being breached or blown up, the garrison was eventually forced to surrender. The survivors, whose number included the celebrated John Knox, were carried off in French ships and put to work as galley-slaves. The castle was later repaired, but its days of active military service were over. Gradually it fell into disrepair and in 1654 the Town Council hastened its demise by ordering that stones from its walls be used to repair the harbour's breakwaters and wharves. But though the structure above the ground has suffered serious depredation, the tunnels in the rock below were fortunately not so easily vandalized, and their hidden history is now revealed to all who wish to explore them.

2 Monastic Secrets

> But what ancient monastery or hall has not its traditional
> subterranean passage?
>
> Allan Fea

Those who accept their own weaknesses as a matter of
course are generally delighted by reports – real or
imaginary – of inappropriate behaviour by individuals
professing adherence to a strict moral code. No group
suffers more keenly from this prurient interest than the
clergy. Almost daily our popular newspapers carry
salacious stories of fallen vicars, devious monks, or nuns
whose behaviour is less spotless than their wimples. From
Chaucer to Umberto Eco writers of fiction have played
upon this fascination with clerical weakness. Monasteries
and abbeys are particularly popular settings for tales of
human frailty and deceit, partly because their inmates
have professed demanding vows, and partly because they
are often closed communities, located in remote corners of
the land.

The plethora of gossip concerning Christian communities presents considerable difficulties to those trying to
separate truth from fiction in the matter of secret hidey
holes and tunnels. As Allan Fea noted almost a century
ago, 'What ancient monastery or hall has not its traditional
subterranean passage?' The problem is exacerbated by the
medieval monks' laudable desire for cleanliness, as a
result of which most monasteries and abbeys were blessed
with sophisticated systems for providing running water
and removing waste. These involved the construction of

an elaborate subterranean network of drains, pipes and tunnels, some of which are still intact. It is these facilities for the promotion of physical wellbeing which have given rise to most of the rumours of moral debility. An underground passage is invariably labelled 'secret' as soon as it is discovered, for popular imagination rejects out of hand all suggestion that it should have been constructed for anything so mundane as the removal of sewage.

In fact, though not always able to maintain the highest moral standards expected of them, most medieval religious houses were, comparatively speaking, havens of rectitude. Moreover, as Henry VIII's blatantly subjective *Valor Ecclesiasticus* made clear, those in religious institutions generally had no need to resort to tunnels in order to slake their thirst for forbidden pleasure. If the sins of Sodom were not to their taste, there were usually plenty of clandestine ways either to introduce members of the opposite sex into the house, or to arrange assignations further afield. It is almost inconceivable that even the most corrupt monastery or nunnery would have gone to the expense and inconvenience of constructing a tunnel merely to provide itself with a secret means of ingress and egress. Nevertheless, fed by popular fiction and gothic films, the stories persist. They are part of our folklore, and no amount of scholarship is ever likely to prevent their circulation.

Beaulieu in Hampshire, home of the world-famous motor museum, is a large and popular complex of buildings constructed within the grounds of an ancient Cistercian foundation. The abbey was served with the usual network of wide underground drains and culverts, the openings to two of which can be viewed in the grounds of the palace. And so, sure enough, there are rumours of passages linking various parts of the estate, though no one is able to explain satisfactorily why the monks should have bothered to dig these tunnels. More interesting is the so-called 'Secret Staircase' within the Great Gatehouse of the abbey. Originally linking an open reception area with the two chapels above, the staircase was abandoned either when the building was converted into a hunting lodge at the time of the dissolution, or during subsequent alterations. It was given the name 'Secret Staircase' by the generations of Montague children who played upon it – no doubt it proved a wonderful way of avoiding the calls of nanny at bathtime.

There are some interesting wall-passages and remote chambers on the second floor of the magnificent gatehouse built to impress visitors to Thornton Abbey, Humberside. No one is quite sure why these cavities were constructed, particularly as some of the little rooms could be entered from the main chamber only by scaling ladders. Perhaps they were intended as quiet refuges where monks could retire to pray in complete silence. If this was the case, then the austerity of the cells contrasts sharply, and reassuringly, with the ostentation of the rest of the building. There is an unsubstantiated legend that in the reign of Queen Elizabeth I the remains of an immured canon were uncovered at Thornton. The skeleton was supposed to have been seated at a desk, with pen and ink before him, but there is no clue as to the room in which the grisly scene was discovered.

Hartland Abbey, which occupies a delightful setting within an area of outstanding natural beauty near Hartland Point in north Devon, was the last of the great religious houses to be dissolved by Henry VIII. The present mansion was raised upon the foundations of a building put up by Augustinian canons in the twelfth century. We are told that as well as building above the ground, the canons also burrowed beneath it, digging a secret tunnel from the bank of the nearby river to St Nectan's Church in the village of Stoke, where they held services. Again, we are not told why the brethren should have taken to tunnelling – surely it cannot have been merely to enable them to get to church in the dry? It is probable that the passage was some sort of drain, although owing to the lack of evidence other purposes cannot be ruled out. The tunnel is no longer in use, but its entrance can be seen beneath a bridge beside the abbey.

Since the murder of Archbishop Thomas à Becket in the late twelfth century, Canterbury has been one of the country's most popular centres of pilgrimage and tourism. The numerous dark corners and sinister openings within the cathedral precincts provide plenty of material for those interested in delving into hidden history. Like many great cathedrals, Canterbury's magnificent complex of crypt, tower, aisle and nave is riddled with intramural stairways and passages. Though these are not strictly secret, for security reasons they are not now open to the general public and few tourists are aware of their existence.

Canterbury is even more mysterious below ground level. On the northern side of the cathedral is a broad lawn known as the Green Court. During the Second World War the area is supposed to have held a large air-raid shelter. When the conflict ended, protruding brick and concrete outworks were demolished and, for financial or pessimistic reasons, the underground parts of the bunker were simply covered with earth and sown with grass. The presence of this secret shelter is said to explain the Court's uneven surface. Tourists visiting the precincts in winter months are sometimes startled to see clouds of steam and smoke issuing from gratings on the southern side of the Green Court, as if some diabolic kitchen was situated deep beneath the ground there. The weird exhalations are in fact only the exhaust of the cathedral's heating plant, hidden from view in a subterranean vault of the old monastery.

This boiler room is only part of a warren of hidden passages and chambers which are said to run beneath the cathedral precincts and the city. There are unsubstantiated reports in Pearson's *Caves and Tunnels of South-East England* of a 'fine late Norman tunnel' beneath the High Street, which had 'a much more important object than mere drainage.' One wonders what that object might have been. Was it an old sally port connected to the Norman castle? Or perhaps the passage was part of the supposed underground link between the Old Palace of the Archbishops of Canterbury near the cathedral (the ruins of which are now incorporated into a boarding house for girls) and the Archbishop's Palace at Bekesbourne, where Cranmer wrote much of the English Prayer Book. Relations between the archbishops and the monastic cathedral were rarely cordial, but it would be surprising if the primate had felt it necessary to resort to a secret passage several kilometers long to ensure a safe entry into his provincial headquarters. Once again, drainage is probably the likeliest explanation for the rumour.

We cannot leave Canterbury without mentioning the most celebrated of all the city's secret chambers which is situated in a sunless vault known as the Dark Entry. The legend of Nell the Cook comes from the reign of Henry VIII, shortly after the dissolution of the monasteries. A lusty canon of the cathedral chapter employed a young lady from the town as his cook. After a while, when the bachelor found that Nell was willing to minister to needs other than strictly nutritional ones, she became his mistress. The relationship was affectionate and Nell soon found herself in love with her handsome employer. One day, however, the man received a visit from his beautiful teenage niece. She was an educated and refined girl, beside whose charms those of the humble cook appeared tawdry and commonplace. It requires little imagination to foresee what happened next.

The niece replaced Nell in the canon's affections, causing the rejected servant to burn with a bitter and jealous hatred. Her revenge was simple and appropriate to her position: she fed her master and his lover a poisoned pie. When the canon failed to appear at the cathedral services the next day, anxious colleagues broke into his locked apartments and found uncle and niece dead upon the bed. Suspicion immediately fell upon poor Nell. A search of the kitchen soon revealed the remains of the poison. For reasons which are never explained, she was not handed over to the civil authorities but condemned to die within the precincts where she had committed her heinous crime.

Beneath a broad slab of stone in the Dark Entry there was, and may still be, a deep, airless vault which had once been part of the cathedral drains. Nell was dragged to this pit, sealed inside and left to die. For a short while afterwards the cloister echoed to the sounds of her sobs and frantic scrabbling. Cathedral employees passed by the spot with hurried steps, or avoided it altogether. Within a few days, however, peace had returned to the hallowed ruins. Time passed, and over the next 300 years Nell the Cook was all but forgotten. Only in tales circulating the city's taverns was the story of the canon and his heartbroken cook kept alive.

And that might have been the end of the story had it not been for a chance discovery by three chapter workmen about a century and a half ago. The men were digging in the Dark Entry when they happened upon Nell's ghastly place of execution. Her skeleton lay crumpled at the bottom of the pit, on the steep sides of which were still visible the deep gouges made by her finger nails as she had tried in vain to claw her way to the surface. And the place was clearly cursed, for within twelve months all three labourers were dead.

Nell's sad spirit still haunts the Dark Entry. It is reported that those who see her consider themselves fortunate if they live to see the year out. Even on a summer's day the tragic cloister has a cold and sinister feel about it. The path is uneven, its cobbles and bricks interspersed with wide paving stones. Goodness knows what secrets lie beneath them.

Most cathedrals which were originally monastic foundations have passages and tunnels similar to those at Canterbury. Winchester, for example, boasts an extensive medieval drainage system known as the Lockburne, and a vaulted tunnel encircling the close carries water from the River Itchen around the precincts. Stoneleigh Abbey in Warwickshire is a grand eighteenth-century mansion unfortunately closed to the public at the moment. It replaced the Elizabethan manor house which was built over the ruins of the original Cistercian abbey. But the medieval foundations remain, and there is a passage leading from a cellar in the private east wing to Pype's Mill, some 2.5 kilometres away. It was almost certainly built as a drain or a conduit for fresh water. Lord Leigh, the present owner of the estate, once explored the first few metres of the tunnel. After a short distance he found that he was able to advance only by crawling. At this point, contemplating a return trip of more than 1800 metres squirming backwards on his stomach, he decided to abort his journey. It comes as no surprise to learn that locals believe the passage to have been used by Abbot de Pype for secret access to his concubines (the fecund father is supposed to have sired more children than there were monks in his abbey).

There is a tunnel beneath the National Trust property of Buckland Abbey in Devon, although it is not open to the public. The large passage discovered in the 1920s beneath St Radigund's Abbey, Kent, unusually did not appear to be connected with the local watercourses, but it is likely that it was used for nothing more sinister than supplying the house with fuel and victuals. The route is now sealed off. At Lavenham Priory in Suffolk a whole network of underground drains has been explored and photographed. There is access from the house to these tunnels, which tourists usually find quite fascinating.

There is an interesting story attached to the lectern in Southwell Minster, Nottinghamshire – a building justly famous for its wonderful medieval stone carvings. The lectern, which is in the traditional form of an eagle perched on a globe, is said to have originally belonged to Newstead Abbey, a priory which stood nearby. The building was converted into the Byron family home in the sixteenth century and now contains a fine collection of Byronic memorabilia. It is not with these, however, that we are concerned at the moment but with the Great Lake, a stretch of water in the abbey grounds.

When the property of the monks, the eagle may have served as a rather grand money box in which the papal tribute known as Peter's Pence was collected. At the time of the dissolution the lectern's double function gave the prior the idea of opening the ball on which the eagle stood and hiding in it the priory's title deeds to keep them out of the hands of the royal commissioners. When the documents had been safely sealed in their casket, the eagle and its perch were thrown into the monk's fishpond. Here they remained for 200 years. They were eventually pulled out of the lake during dredging undertaken by the fifth Lord Byron. The lectern and a number of other small items were then sold to Sir Richard Kaye. It was only when the brass was being cleaned that a servant noticed that there was something within the hollow globe. It was promptly forced open, and out fell the deeds, as dry and intact as on the day when they had been hidden.

We now move from the world of historical actuality into the realm of legend. Nevertheless, tourists may care to visit some of the places mentioned below, either in the hope of noticing something which others have missed, or just to savour the atmosphere which has given rise to speculation.

Our first call is at Iford Manor, near Bradford-on-Avon in Wiltshire. The owner regrets that no secret passage has been found in either the house or the garden; but both inside and outside the manor a pleasant smell of incense can be noticed, quite at random, and at any time of the year. There was a monastery nearby in the Middle Ages, and for a while Iford was the home of a Roman Catholic family, so there just may be a tunnel or secret room somewhere around, waiting to be discovered.

The evidence for secret ways beneath the ancient abbey at Bury St Edmunds, Suffolk, is more concrete, for the house was certainly served by an adequate drainage system. This is supposed to run below the houses which were built on to the abbey ruins. In the fifteenth century they were said to have been used by the sinister nun Maude Carew, whom legend holds responsible for the death by poisoning of Humphrey, Duke of Gloucester.

Other abbeys and priories which in the past have been listed as sites of mysterious tunnels are Glastonbury (where the passage went from the abbey to the George and Pilgrims Inn), St Albans, Worcester, Lincoln, Fountains and Bath, where a conduit leading from the Abbey Church House was found in 1856. It might have been constructed to bring the famous spa waters to the leper colony which in the twelfth century occupied the position later adopted by the monks. It is worth mentioning here that Bath Abbey is one of the few ecclesiastical buildings to contain a genuinely secret room. In the early fifteenth century the robing room of Bishop King was walled up. When it was rediscovered in the eighteenth century the bishop's vestments were found hanging on the wall, just as he had left them 300 years before. Unfortunately, when fresh air was admitted into the chamber they disintegrated before steps could be taken to preserve them.

Those seeking a haunted tunnel might try the Coopers' Arms in Rochester. The pub is said to have been built on the site of a priory from which tunnels (drains again!) led to the river. The benevolent ghost of a bricked-up monk has been seen amid the barrels and crates of the cellar, though the siting may owe more to the distorting effects of the liquors stored around his haunt than to a genuine presence.

Legend tells of a secret passage linking Scotney Castle in Kent with Bayham Abbey, about 4 kilometres away. Locals once tested the veracity of the story by sending a dog down one end of the tunnel and then waiting to see where it came out. Days passed. Eventually, a week later, the animal appeared at the other end of the tunnel. But no one could be persuaded to follow in the animal's footsteps, for in the course of its journey the poor creature had lost every single hair from its back. Another Kentish story talks of an underground castle–abbey link at Leeds, but neither man nor beast has been able to trace it.

With the supposed exploits of the hermit Cistercians at Forde Abbey in Somerset our long catalogue of clandestine monastic chicanery must come to a close. The original abbey buildings still stand, transformed in the sixteenth and seventeenth centuries into a most elegant country house. The monks farmed the land around the monastery, working closely with the local communities. Just how close this relationship was, we do not know. Some say the brothers had families secreted away in neighbouring farmsteads. Almost inevitably, this supposition gave rise to legends of tunnels running from the abbey to the buildings where the monks' children lived.

It is not only the religious and military buildings of the Middle Ages which are associated with secret passages and chambers. A large number of ancient domestic dwellings have similar connections. Once again, however, we are faced with the problem of differentiating fact from legend. To illustrate this, perhaps we should begin our tour with the charming Tudor manor house at Avebury in Wiltshire, supposedly the most haunted house in the country.

In Norman times the Benedictines founded a priory at Avebury, near the site of the present manor. After the dissolution of the monasteries in the later 1530s, the estate was sold to Sir William Sharrington, who ran the Bristol Mint for Henry VIII. At a time when the coinage was subject to officially sanctioned debasement and even the best-kept books were by modern standards inadequate, the position was both literally and metaphorically a licence to produce money. Sir William made the most of his opportunities and assembled a considerable fortune by clipping coins, melting down Church plate and keeping two sets of Mint accounts: false ones for official purposes, and the true figures for personal use. Eventually the fraud was discovered and the corrupt official sentenced to death. He seems to have been saved by the change of regime occasioned by the death of the king in 1547. More interested in cash than justice, the pragmatic government of Protector Somerset granted Sir William a pardon on payment of a fine of £12,000. To a council at war with both France and Scotland this large sum of money was clearly of greater practical use than a severed head. Chastened and rather less well-off, the lord of Avebury Manor returned to his estates and lived to be appointed High Sheriff of Wiltshire a year or two later.

Local legend insists that Sir William Sharrington never revealed the full extent of his fortune, but hid most of the treasure he had accumulated somewhere in the manor or its garden. It is said that if one stands with one's back against the east wall in the south-east garden, 1.8 metres from the Rose Garden wall, then takes twenty-two paces to the west, one will end up directly over the entrance to a tunnel. The supposed passage dates from the time of the priory, and links the main house to the nearby church of St James's. Although the detailed instructions on how to locate the secret way appear to come straight from Victorian romantic fiction, there may well be a medieval drain in the vicinity. If Sir William really did have to hide his illicit fortune in a hurry, the disused sewer would undoubtably have made a secure repository for one living before the advent of discreet Swiss bank accounts.

The Sharrington treasure may alternatively be hidden within the manor itself. An Australian lady visiting the house in 1989 caused quite a commotion by pausing before the fireplace in the Queen Anne Room and announcing with unabashed certainty that there was something behind it. She declared that the fixture and the space behind it had been revealed to her in a dream. She was not sure what the mysterious cavity held, and Ken King, the owner of the manor, is loth to sanction the expense and disruption involved in dismantling the fireplace on such uncertain evidence. If one day he undertakes the task, perhaps the riddle of the missing fortune will be solved.

Tourists who sample Avebury's 'Elizabethan Experience' – the manor's catchy slogan – will also notice three secret doors on the Cavalier Landing. These lead to the Prayer Room, the Crimson Room (also known as the Cavalier Room) and the back staircase. The latter is haunted by one of the site's numerous ghosts, a White Lady who has also been seen lending a hand by guiding visitors round the garden. Other spectral residents include a monk who wanders about the South Library, and Sir John Stowell, a Royalist officer who makes his presence felt by unlocking the cupboards in the Cavalier Room and strewing rose petals on the floor.

Layer Marney Tower, Essex, is another building able to provide plenty of ghost stories, though more interesting as far as we are concerned is the entrance in the cellars to a secret tunnel leading to Tiptree Priory or nearby Duke's Farm. Unfortunately, however, the nether regions of the Tower are not open to public view. Tourists looking for hidden history will have more joy at the Bull House near Barnstaple in Devon, once the domestic quarters of Pilton Priory. In a tiny chamber next to an oak-panelled room visitors can be shown two loose floorboards, beneath which an underground passage is clearly visible. It is a well-constructed barrel vault, almost 2 metres high and more than 1 metre wide. Stories abound about it being used in medieval times for facilitating liasons between monks and nuns. But since there was no religious house for ladies in the vicinity, a more prosaic explanation for the passage is likely. This was confirmed over a century ago when a party exploring the vault was forced to turn back, 'stopped by foul air' (from Fea's *Secret Chambers and Hiding Places*).

The fact that almost all the so-called 'secret tunnels' in medieval residences were built for sanitation does not preclude the builders having had more glamorous secondary functions in mind. The problem is that we usually have no concrete evidence for drains being used for other purposes. The wide tunnels beneath the Manor House at Chenies in Hertfordshire, for example, may well have been designed to enable those in the house to escape into an adjoining wood should the need arise. Similar motives may have dictated the large size of the drainage passages beneath Braemore House in Hampshire and Gawsworth Hall in Cheshire. (It should be made clear at this point that though all these fascinating houses are open to the public, the subterranean works are not visible, and the proprietors would not wish visitors to start delving below ground on their own initiative.) Other ancient houses open to the public which are rumoured to be served by secret tunnels of some description include Poundisford Park (Taunton, Somerset), the Lord Leycester Hospital (Warwickshire), Whittington Court (Gloucestershire), Ludford House (Shropshire), Cadhay (Devon), Hall Place (Kent), Oakwell Hall (West Yorkshire) and Godolphin House (Cornwall). They all certainly merit a visit, but not in the hope of being introduced to anything more secret than the occasional latrine.

Those who really wish to see medieval sewage disposal at its most sophisticated should call at the wonderfully preserved Gainsborough Old Hall, Lincolnshire. The house boasts a fascinating array of privies, chutes and pits, some lit up for closer inspection. The Hall has a number of other interesting nooks and crannies, which will be dealt with in a later chapter. At this point attention may be drawn to the three small rooms in the corners of the kitchen, each with a chamber above accessible only by ladder. No doubt these were simply storerooms, but they would have proved useful refuges for idle or ill-treated kitchen staff.

There is an unusual underground passage beneath the Tudor Hall at Dodington in Somerset. It runs the length of the house, with a flight of steps leading into it from either end. No one knows why it was constructed. Some say that it was put in during Victorian times as a means of combating rising damp; others venture more far-fetched explanations. Leading from this passage is a cellar containing a large copper water-wheel which turned the spit in the kitchen above. There is a more genuine hidey hole at Hellen's, Much Marcle in remote Herefordshire, one of the oldest historic homes in England. The hide, which is clearly visible in the chimney of the chapel, can still be negotiated, and the custodian of the house hopes that one day it will be made safe enough for visitors to explore. The history of the 'escape hole', as it is called, is unknown. As at Dodington, visitors can draw their own conclusions.

The most remarkable piece of hidden medieval architectural history is to be found at Wingfield College, Suffolk. In the late Middle Ages this large timber-framed house was a flourishing boarding school. At the time of the Reformation it passed into the hands of the crown and thence indirectly to the Bishops of Norwich. Towards the close of the eighteenth century Squire Buck decided that the old building was no longer suitable accommodation. Instead of pulling it down, however, for some reason he chose to hide it almost entirely beneath Georgian 'improvements', including a Palladian facade, false walls, ceilings and floors. Thus the medieval structure vanished from view, and only in 1971 did the owner, Ian Chance, discover the unique treasure lying beneath the shell of his home. Since that time much of the original building has been revealed and restored. Wingfield is now a successful college of arts and music. It is well worth a visit, for nowhere else will the reader find not merely a secret room or passage, but a whole house which had been hidden from view for almost 200 years.

3   Elusive Recusants

Great joy was caused all through the kingdom by the arrest
of Owen, knowing his skill in constructing hiding-places,
and the innumerable number of these dark holes which he
had schemed for hiding priests throughout the kingdom.

Robert Cecil

Scotney Old Castle near Lamberhurst, close to Kent's
south-western border with Sussex, is one of the most
picturesque ruins in the south of England. The moated
and broken monument, half-castle, half-manor house,
stands amid the delightful landscaped gardens which
were created in the mid-nineteenth century to enhance
the setting of the nearby Salvin mansion. A steep scarp,
patterned with flower beds, rhododendron bushes, shrubs
and majestic trees, sweeps down to the edge of the
lily-strewn still water which reflects the old stone of the
castle against the changing southern skies. Only the
fragmented chatter of visitors and the constant clicking of
their camera shutters encroach on the pastoral tranquillity
of this most perfect piece of English romanticism. But it
was not always thus. Four hundred years ago the peaceful
rhythms of daily life at Scotney were suddenly and rudely
broken.

The Darell family acquired the remote castle in 1411. In
the late sixteenth century Thomas Darell II reconstructed
the south wing of his ancestral home, incorporating in the
new work several secret hiding places. Thomas was a
Roman Catholic, a recusant. Whether he liked it or not, his

adherence to the faith of the Counter-Reformation had political repercussions. During the 1580s England's relations with Catholic Spain, the dominant power in Western Europe, were fast deteriorating towards open warfare and the famous Armada campaign of 1588. The next year Queen Elizabeth's government sought to take advantage of the temporary set-back which they had inflicted on their enemy by launching a large expedition against Portugal (then a Spanish satellite) and the Azores. The over-ambitious scheme ended in disaster. Many English soldiers perished in the arid countryside around Lisbon. Some were taken prisoner, and the remnants of the ill-prepared and poorly-led expedition limped home to England in the autumn. The queen was displeased.

Over the next couple of years some of the men who had been captured during the summer campaign of 1589 managed to find their way back to England. Always on the look out for spies and Catholic priests, the government was suspicious of such escapees and subjected them to close questioning before they were allowed to collect the bounty due to them. This was the case with a group which came ashore in the spring of 1591. Two of their number, Richard Blount and James Younger, were taken before the Lord High Admiral, Lord Howard of Effingham, and carefully examined. The refugees had prepared carefully for such an eventuality. They knew the details of the campaign and were even able to help the Admiral by furnishing him with some (incorrect) information on the deployment of Spanish forces. Eventually the men were congratulated on their good fortune and released. Thus the number of Roman Catholic missionaries at work in England rose by two.

Richard Blount was a Jesuit. A well-educated man of middle height with a large auburn beard, he made his way to the secluded safety of Scotney, where he served the Catholic cause for seven years. Eventually, however, his presence was betrayed to the authorities by an informer, or 'pursuivant', the contemporary term for one who made it his job to hunt out Catholic priests. Warned of the approach of a search party, Blount and his servant Bray hid 'in a secret place under a stair' (Morris, *Troubles of Our Catholic Forefathers*). This tiny hide, which was redi-scovered in 1860, lies beneath a space under the eaves and is entered through a door leading from the staircase put in by Thomas Darrel in 1580. It is only just large enough to accommodate two men, so the deprivations and squalor endured by Blount and his man in 1597 must have been extreme. They hid there for a week.

The search was conducted by two magistrates, a pursuivant and sundry guards and workmen. When carrying out a thorough investigation of a house it was necessary to bring along carpenters, masons and others skilled in the construction industry, for only they had sufficient expertise to disclose false walls or beams and to reveal the unexplained discrepancies between internal and external measurements which often betrayed a concealed space. Like most detective work, hunting for a priest hole was more an intellectual exercise than a physical one. Pursuivants who thundered about a house, smashing panels at random and peering into the most obvious dark corners, rarely found what they were looking for. Successful searchers set about assembling their evidence systematically and methodically, working through one room at a time, tapping, measuring and stripping away decoration. Evidence thus gathered was then analysed to see if it afforded any clues as to the whereabouts of a hide. While this work was going on the hunters had to keep one ear open for possible noises issuing from within a secret space, such as a cough or even the sounds made by a priest exercising his normal bodily functions (toilet arrangements within a hide always posed an unpleasant problem).

Where possible, raids were made with a minimum of warning. This was done in order to catch a recusant priest before he had time to conceal himself, or, failing that, before he could be provided with adequate food and drink to sustain him through a long search. However, since Catholic priests usually sheltered in the large and securely barred houses of the gentry, it was unusual for a search party to burst straight in. Even where this might have been practicable, pursuivants rarely felt able to force their way into the household of a social superior. A property under suspicion was first isolated then kept under close guard, particularly at night, lest the quarry slip out undetected. On several occasions guards failed in their duty owing to fatigue or over-consumption of alcohol (an interesting comment on Tudor and Jacobean drinking habits). Finally, the government officers had to keep their wits about them. As we shall see in the story of two searches at Scotney, the recusants were capable of employing all kinds of tricks to put the hunters off the scent.

Those looking for Father Blount followed most of the rules of the chase. Thomas Darell was sent to London, where he was locked in Newgate prison. His wife was housed with the family of one of the magistrates, and all but one of the servants were temporarily secured in the county jail. A maid was permitted to stay in the castle to look after the younger children, whom the magistrates considered too innocent to come under suspicion. William Darell, one of those left in the house, later wrote an account of what had happened. Having thus cleared the house of anyone who might interfere with their activities, the search party then set to work. Though we cannot be certain, it is unlikely that they got as far as taking measurements in the roof space where the Catholic pair were concealed, for had they done so they would almost certainly have uncovered the hide. As it turned out, starvation and not skill brought the search to an end.

After seven days in the cold, cramped hide Blount and his servant could take no more. When the pursuivants were in another part of the house, Bray crept out of the hiding place, secured it behind him, and gave himself up with a concocted story of how he came to be there. When the magistrates demanded to know where he had been concealed, Bray showed them another hide which, fortunately for him, the officers had also failed to locate. The servant was taken away for questioning, and Blount escaped. It was soon obvious to the magistrates that their prisoner was no priest and clearly not the man they had been looking for. Bray was released after a stern warning, and soon rejoined his master. Thwarted but not defeated, the officers of the law determined to wait for the Scotney household to return to normal, then strike again.

The second raid took place at Christmas 1598. This time the pursuivants were certain that their quarry was within the castle, for they had been tipped off by a servant named Henbury. There is no mention of Thomas Darell being present at Scotney on this occasion. Since he died at some time during 1598, it has been suggested that he had perished as a result of the deprivations suffered in Newgate.

The search party came to the house in the middle of the night and surrounded it, waiting until dawn before they made their approach. At first light they spotted a housemaid who had risen early to light the fires. Having forced their way into the house with the terrified girl, they commanded her to light a candle and lead them to the main bedroom. By this time it had dawned on the maid that it was not robbers who had apprehended her but pursuivants. Instead of leading the men directly upstairs, she stood at the bottom and called to her mistress that three justices and a large party of their men had called to see her. The girl's quick thinking saved the priest's life.

Roused by the noise, Blount and Bray gathered together all their popish stuff, pulled on a few clothes, and scampered barefoot into a 'secret place, digged in a thick stone wall' at the foot of a small turret some distance from the main part of the house. (The exact location of the hiding place is now lost.) Swinging shut the stone slab which acted as a door to their hiding place, the two men sat panting in the darkness for a few minutes before taking stock of their position. For the second time in a year they found themselves incarcerated together at perilously short notice. It was mid-winter and bitterly cold. Neither man had shoes, and Bray was wearing nothing but his breeches. In their rush to get into the hide they had managed to take only a bottle of wine and a loaf of bread – singularly appropriate nourishment for a priest, one might think, but hardly sufficient to sustain two men for any length of time. The pair did not regard their future prospects with much joy. Their fears would have been even greater had they realized what they had done on entering the cell: in their haste to shut the door they had left the tasseled end of a girdle hanging outside between the stones.

Meanwhile, back in the house, the pursuivants were setting about their business. Mrs Darell and her children were locked in the gatehouse and, presumably, most of the servants were taken away. Sir George Rivers and his fellow justices then organized the search. We are told that the operation continued for ten days. It is difficult to believe that Blount and Bray could have survived that long under the terrible conditions of their hide. Either the search was conducted more quickly, or, more likely in the light of what had happened previously, Mrs Darrel had arranged for the hide to be stocked with a few provisions and blankets. It is hard to see how else two half-naked men could have sat in a hole in a wall for ten days in December, then emerged fit enough to perform remarkable athletic feats.

After several days' fruitless activity the pursuivants called off the hunt and released Mrs Darell, though they remained in the house and kept a discreet watch on its inhabitants. Believing herself to be unobserved, in the late afternoon the mistress of the household took a walk round the castle grounds. At length she made her way to the court where the hide was situated. Here, to her horror, she noticed the end of the girdle. Without attracting attention to her action, she moved over to the spot and succeeded in cutting off the offending tassle, leaving only a stub of cord projecting through the stonework. 'Pull in the string', she hissed. After a short delay the line duly disappeared into the crevice. Mrs Darrell turned to walk back to the house.

At this point she saw one or two pursuivants standing nearby. They had not seen her cut the cord, but they had heard her whisper and 'asked her to whom she spake and of what string'. The explanation she gave was in the circumstances hardly plausible: she said that she was calling to someone to open the latch of a door through which she wished to pass.

Before long heavy instruments had been summoned and workmen were beating at the stones of the wall, seeing if one of them appeared loose and listening for any sound of hollowness within. Though the searchers were still not certain that they had uncovered a hide, Blount and Bray could see no way of escape. When the hinges of the door began to give way, they put their backs against it to stop it moving and to muffle the echoes. Already through the chinks in the stonework they could see the light of the candles which the workmen were holding. Then, just when it seemed certain that the door would give way and the men be led off into captivity, the noise stopped. It had started to rain. Soon torrents of water were gushing from the gargoyles at the wall head directly on to the labourers below. Cursing, they threw down their implements and went indoors to dry out and take a drink by the fire. The search was called off until the morning, and two guards were placed at the entrance to the courtyard.

The recusant pair could scarcely believe their good fortune (or 'act of God's Providence', as one Catholic source, Morris's *Troubles of Our Catholic Forefathers*, puts it). They crept from their lair, closed the door behind them and hid all incriminating Catholic evidence in the moat. This done, they moved stealthily to the castle's ruined south-eastern tower and scrambled to the top. The moat lay icy and black below them.

It is at this point that the story begins to lose most of its credibility. We are told that Blount wished to plunge into the water and tow Bray, who was unable to swim, to the other side. If this was the plan, then why had they climbed a tower? The moment was hardly appropriate for diving practice, and leaping into the moat from a height would only increase the chances of the sound of their escape being detected by the guards. Be that as it may, we are told that Blount directed his servant to a point where the moat could be forded, then, handing over his cassock, he jumped into the water and swam 22 metres to the other side. From here, clad only in soaking wet breeches, he struck out across the fields into the darkness. But he had not gone far before he realized that he was lost. Hearing a great commotion in the castle, he stealthily made his way back there and hid among the trees, waiting for Bray.

As soon as he had seen his master take to the water, the resourceful servant had started to creep towards the shallow section of the moat. Scotney Castle occupies two islands. The place that Bray needed to get to was on the one furthest from him, across a narrow causeway guarded by a gatehouse. To his dismay he found that the gates of the portal were locked shut. Undaunted, he wrapped Blount's cloak tightly around him and

> boldly came into the hall, where he found a great company lying asleep, and boldly cries, 'Thieves, thieves in the stable! Drunken rogues, do you lie here and suffer my master, Sir George Rivers' horses to be stolen?' At which they roused up, all of them crying, 'Thieves, thieves in the stable!' And running and crying, the two men in the court opened the gate, and let them out, and Bray with them.
>
> (Morris, *Troubles of Our Catholic Forefathers*)

It was a desperate ruse, but it worked. The men must have thought that it was the priest who was among the horses. Only when they reached the stables and found all the animals standing peacefully in their stalls did it occur to them to question more closely the shadowy figure who had raised the alarm. But by that time Bray was nowhere to be found. Taking advantage of the confusion, he had splashed across the moat and joined his master. The two men were now far away.

Blount never returned to Scotney. After receiving a change of clothes and some food at a friendly farm in the neighbourhood, that night the priest and his servant put another 22 kilometres between themselves and their pursuers. Early the next morning, while the refugees were begging breakfast from a startled milkmaid, the search party at Scotney discovered the hide and began scouring the surrounding countryside. They even dragged the moat in the hope of finding the priest's body. Eventually they gave up and withdrew from the castle. By this time Blount was in London, where he spent the remaining forty years of his life discreetly ministering to the Catholic community of the capital.

The extraordinary events at Scotney Castle cannot be fully understood without realizing how the English government viewed Roman Catholicism in the late sixteenth century. The situation arose from the remarkable changes which began about seventy years before. The position of the medieval Church is without parallel today. It was an enormously powerful international institution, owning huge tracts of land, controlling most education and learning, and wielding vast power through its own system of courts. It touched the people of Europe at every point in their lives, literally from the cradle to the grave. And, of course, an organization of such magnitude and wealth possessed considerable political influence. The repercussions of a split in the Church, which originated in Germany with the teachings of Martin Luther, reverberated round the continent for hundreds of years.

The Reformation in England followed a hesitant and erratic course. It began when Henry VIII renounced papal authority and seized much of the Church's wealth, calling himself Supreme Head of a national Church. Protestant doctrinal changes followed during the reign of his son, Edward VI (1547–53), but had little time to take root before Queen Mary I (1553–8) attempted to lead the country back to Rome. There is much controversy among scholars about the extent to which the several Acts of Parliament altered the faith and day to day practices of ordinary citizens. Much depended upon the vigour of local authorities, so that in many parts of the land, especially in the north and west, religious belief probably changed only slowly. There may have been casual conformity to the changing commands from the centre, but most men and women knew little of theology, and the religion which had served the country for almost a thousand years would not wither away merely as a result of laws issuing from Westminster.

Elizabeth I (1558–1603) was above all a politician. She is

supposed to have declared that she had no wish to 'make
windows into mens' souls'; but as the daughter of Henry
VIII and Anne Boleyn, whose union had first brought
about the breach with Rome, she had little choice but to
pursue a Protestant course. The religious settlement of
1559 declared the queen to be the Supreme Governor of
the English Church, the Protestant framework of which
was established by an Act of Uniformity, Royal
Injunctions and the Thirty-Nine Articles. This develop-
ment was clearly alarming for the Catholic community. In
Elizabethan England religion and politics were inextri-
cably entwined: one could not deny the authority of the
Church of England without thereby implicitly rejecting
the authority of the queen – and to do that was treason.
For about nine years, however, there was a sort of phoney
war. The recusancy fines of one shilling a month were
haphazardly collected. The government seemed more
concerned with coming to grips with the fissiparous
activities of puritan fellow Protestants, who wished to see
the Church stripped of all remaining traces of popery,
than with persecuting a relatively quiescant and shrinking
Catholic minority. The plight of the Catholics was not
helped by the inactivity of Rome, which delayed declaring
Elizabeth a heretic in the hope that she might return to
Rome of her own accord. If there was any real chance of
bringing England back to the Catholic fold, it was during
these early years of Elizabeth's reign, when the new
national Church had few strong supporters and the old
religion was not associated closely in people's minds with
political upheaval. The papal Bull *Regnans in Excelsis*
(1570), which decreed the queen's excommunication and
deposition, arrived too late.

The Roman Catholic Mary Queen of Scots had arrived
in northern England in 1568, thereby providing the
necessary stimulus and focus for the unsuccessful Revolt
of the Northern Earls the next year. This rebellion,
together with the Papal Bull and the Ridolfi Plot to depose
Elizabeth and put her cousin Mary on the throne,
hardened English attitudes towards the Catholics.
Between 1571 and 1597 the laws against them were

strengthened on at least five separate occasions, increas-
ing the recusancy fines to an exorbitant £20 a month and
declaring guilty of treason not only Jesuits and seminary
priests, but also those who received them. Pursuivants
were furnished with two sharp new weapons from the
legal armoury: a suspected papist who failed to present
himself for trial could be found guilty of recusancy in his
absence; and the forked 'Bloody Question' was drawn up
for putting to suspects: would they defend England
against forces led by the Pope himself?

Historians tend to distinguish between the religious and
the political threat of Roman Catholicism, though little
such distinction guided the thoughts of the Elizabethan
government and the majority of MPs. For them the
religion of Rome meant plots on behalf of the Queen of
Scots to assassinate Elizabeth. The scheme of 1571 was
followed by another in 1583 and the Babington Plot three
years later, as a result of which the queen was finally
persuaded to agree to the execution of her Franco-Scottish
rival. Catholicism was also forcefully proselytized by
Spain, with whom England found herself at war in 1585
and who launched three armadas against the country. By
the mid-1580s English fear of popery was quite as great
(and often as irrational) as American antipathy towards
communism during the period of the Cold War.

The Catholic religious threat came from missionary
priests like Father Blount, trained abroad and sent to
England to bring the country back to Rome. The first
college to educate such men was established at Douai in
the Netherlands in 1568, moving to Rheims ten years later.
In 1579 an English Jesuit college was established in Rome.
The first secular priest arrived in 1574 and the first Jesuits
in 1580. In response to the threat the government formed a
Corps of Pursuivants, men who made it their job to track
down Catholic missionary priests. A successful member of
the Corps could accumulate considerable wealth in
reward for his services. A total of 649 priests were sent to
England during Elizabeth's reign, of whom 125 were
executed for treason between 1585 and 1603. A further
fifty-five lay persons were executed over the same period.

The government always insisted that, unlike Queen Mary's regime, it was persecuting people not for their faith but for owing allegiance to a hostile foreign power at a time of national emergency.

Inspiring though the story of the Catholic priests may be, from a practical point of view their campaign was seriously flawed. Often from respectable social backgrounds themselves, they concentrated their efforts too much on the gentry, largely ignoring the needs of the considerable number of humbler Catholics without whose support it was not possible to create a large-scale Catholic renaissance. The priests also paid too much attention to the strongly Protestant south-east, where they stood little chance of making much headway, instead of seeking to expand from their power bases in the north and west. The work of Father Blount in Kent and London is a good example of this misguided strategy. In the priests' defence, however, it may be argued that only the gentry were powerful enough to succour them, and there was little point in their operating in a county like Lancashire where the faith was still quite deeply rooted.

More serious was the difference in attitude between the priests and most of their lay co-religionists. As the reaction of secular Catholics to the advent of the Spanish Armada made clear, they did not see themselves as traitors. They were not missionaries, but wished merely to preserve their comfortable 'seigneurial Catholicism' as part of a traditional way of life, without political strings. Few Catholic gentry saw themselves as potential leaders of a revolution, though they did believe that they were the papists' natural leaders. Most wished to be left in peace to worship God in the manner to which they had become accustomed. The priests, on the other hand, were men who had taken the decision to devote their lives to spearheading the restoration of Catholicism in England. They were fired by a burning zeal and were prepared to risk torture and death for their cause. Some were quite prepared to accept foreign aid, military or otherwise, if it helped them to accomplish their mission. This division in the Catholic ranks became apparent in the 1590s, emerging in an internecine struggle known as the Archpriest Controversy. It was this which persuaded the English government to draw a distinction between Jesuits and secular priests, and approach the latter with an offer of terms if they would swear allegiance to the Crown.

This, briefly, is the background to the Blount adventure at Scotney and the explanation for the priest holes which can still be seen in dark corners of so many great houses dotted about the kingdom. Romantic though these features may appear today, they were built with deadly serious intent to save lives. Moreover, lest we think the story to be simply one of innocent priests sheltering from the clutches of a cruel government, it is worth recalling that many hides were built by and for members of the Society of Jesus, whose teachings threatened to undermine the very fabric of the Elizabethan state. The avowed long-term intent of many Jesuit priests was to see the queen dead and a Catholic monarch in her place on the throne, helped there, if necessary, by Spanish or French troops. Priest holes, therefore, are a reminder not of a gruesome struggle of good versus evil, but of the unhappy consequences of discarding toleration, that most civilised of all virtues.

The best collection of priest holes in a single building is to be found at Harvington Hall, an attractive moated manor in Worcestershire. The Hall's director, Michael Hodgetts, has made a life-long study of religious hides, and his book *Secret Hiding Places* is an invaluable companion for all those who wish to make a detailed study of the subject. (The present work attempts to do no more than introduce the tourist to some of the more interesting sites which are open to the public.) At Harvington we also encounter for the first time the work of the Jesuit lay brother Nicholas Owen, undoubtably the master-craftsman of priest holes.

Owen was an Oxfordshire man, born into a devout Roman Catholic family sometime during the middle years of the century. His father was a carpenter, which explains how Nicholas came by his detailed knowledge of house construction. He was arrested on several occasions and eventually died under torture in the Tower of London, following the round-up of Catholic priests and other suspects after the 1605 Gunpowder Plot. Father John Gerard, one of Owen's contemporaries, has left us with the following glowing eulogy on Owen's work:

> His chief employment was in making of secret places to hide priests and church stuff from the fury of the searches. In which kind he was so skilful, both to devise and frame the places in the best manner, and his help therein desired in so many places, that I verily think no man can be said to have done more good of all those that laboured in the English vineyard. For, first, he was the immediate occasion of saving the lives of many hundreds of persons both ecclesiastical and secular.

While members of the Elizabethan Privy Council would hardly have described 'Little John' Owen's ingenious work in these terms, he was clearly a remarkably skilled craftsman. It has been estimated that during his career he constructed hides in no less than thirty-five houses. The advantage of being introduced to his handiwork at Harvington is that the Hall possesses no less than eight hides, four pre-Owen ones and four created by the master himself, enabling visitors to compare Owen's skills with those of his predecessors.

The early hides comprise an opening for storing massing stuff under the floor of the chapel (an obvious hiding place if ever there was one); a square hole, large enough for a single man, beside the chimney in the ground floor parlour and entered through a trapdoor in the passage from the withdrawing room to the room over the gateway; a space beneath the privy (a very common position for a hidey hole) beside the South Room; and a small space in a gable above the nursery. A reasonably canny group of pursuivants could probably have uncovered all these places in a day or so. It would have taken them several weeks, however, to discover the other four hides.

Michael Hodgetts suggests that the Owen priest holes were put in at the same time as the great staircase, probably in the first five years of the seventeenth century. They were added as a result of the Archpriest Controversy, which had precluded secular priests from using the Jesuit hides at nearby Hindlip. It has been suggested that in order to carry out the major reconstruction the house was vacated for several weeks so that as few people as possible were privy to the new arrangements.

The construction of the new priest holes certainly involved considerable changes to the interior of the house. False ceilings were inserted below a long corridor known as the Nine Worthies Passage; a dummy fireplace was inserted in the Marble Room providing an escape hatch from the second floor to the garrets; and a large hide was created in the roof, above the Priest's Room. The most cunningly contrived hidey hole was situated in the centre of the house, in a room known as Dr Dodd's library. The entrance to the hide is a massive oak beam, pivoted near the top so that if pressed firmly in the correct place it swings forwards to open a narrow doorway. The most striking hallmark of Owen's work is what one might term double concealment – wherever possible he provided his priest holes with inner and outer walls, so that pursuivants lifting floorboards above a concealed space, for example, would find not the hide itself but an innocuous-looking void. Owen employed just such a trick to protect the hide beneath the Worthies Passage at Harvington.

Oxburgh Hall in Norfolk possesses one of the earliest examples of an Owen hide. The house is a fine example of a fifteenth-century moated manor house, graced with a splendid brick-built twin-towered gateway. During the reign of Elizabeth the Hall was owned by a Catholic gentleman named Thomas Bedingfeld, who lived near the Jesuit district headquarters at Grimston. Bedingfeld probably employed Owen at some point in 1589. (At this time Owen was employed by the prudent leader of the English Jesuits, Father Henry Garnet, from whose service the craftsman must have been granted temporary release). The master of concealed construction created two hides at

Reigate Castle is now little more than grassy mounds strewn with a few shattered pieces of stonework. This modern pyramid marks the entrance to the Barons' Cave, where, according to legend, rebel nobles met in 1215 to put the finishing touches to the Magna Carta.

The entrance to the tunnel in the cellars of Filching Manor. It leads downhill towards the floor of the valley and has yet to be explored thoroughly – escape route, smugglers' passage, or merely a drain?

(*Left*) The keep of Rochester Castle, showing clearly the rounded tower built to replace the original Norman construction which was brought down in 1215 by the sappers of King John's army. The fat from forty pigs was used to fire the props which supported the roof of the mine beneath the tower.

(*Bottom left*) Canterbury's majestic cathedral from the Green Court, with the 'Dark Entry' on the left. Beneath the cathedral precincts run numerous drains which once served the medieval monastery. As with many similar sites, these have given rise to groundless rumours of sinful monks creeping unnoticed into the adjoining town.

(*Bottom right*) Canterbury Cathedral: the entrance to the 'Dark Entry', a long, gloomy passage running through the ruins of the former monastery. The path is said to be haunted still by the sad ghost of Nell Cook.

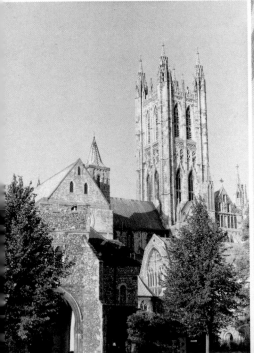

Avebury Manor, Wiltshire, seen from the house's charming walled rose garden. Somewhere in the vicinity the ill-gotten treasure of Sir William Sharrington, Keeper of the Royal Mint at Bristol during the reign of Henry VIII, lies buried in a secret tunnel.

Scotney Old Castle, Kent, the scene of one of the most remarkable priest hunts of Elizabethan times. Father Richard Blount, the hero of the adventure, eventually made his escape from the castle by diving half naked into the icy moat and swimming to the opposite bank.

(*Left*) A small hidey hole in the floor of the chapel at Harvington Hall. It is an early hide, not well concealed but easily accessible and suitable for the rapid concealment of Roman Catholic massing stuff.

(*Bottom left*) One of the most ingenious priest holes of all: the entrance to the Dodd's Library hide, Harvington Hall, was sealed by this pivoted beam. When the 'door' was secured in position only the most meticulous or fortunate pursuivant had any hope of discovering the hide's whereabouts.

(*Bottom right*) A specially made glass panel covering a latrine shaft at Baddesley Clinton. The opening led into a huge priest hole running along the side of the house just above the level of the moat. In 1591 ten men hid in this dank pit for four hours while pursuivants ransacked the house above them.

Latrine chutes were frequently and easily converted into hides, although as we can see from the rather obvious ring projecting from the floor of the sacristy at Baddesley Clinton (Warwickshire), their new function was not always well concealed.

Filching Manor, East Sussex, a medieval building of much mystery. It boasts a tunnel and a priest hole, and may also conceal a secret room and an entrance to a subterranean smugglers' hide.

The lovely Jacobean mansion of Chastleton House, Oxfordshire. For some reason a hidden room was incorporated into the original design – the upper row of panes in the window on the left of the doorway is purely decorative.

Chastleton's secret bedroom in which Captain Arthur Jones hid from Parliamentarian troops after the Battle of Worcester, 1651. The window which now lights the room is a later addition.

A view from the Moat Room of one of the priest holes at Baddesley Clinton, Warwickshire. The original entrance to the hide was via an innocuous-looking fireplace in the Great Parlour.

Oxburgh, one of which was so well hidden that it was not found until the Great Hall was demolished towards the end of the eighteenth century.

The entrance to the extant hide at Oxburgh lies off the King's Room in the gatehouse, though this was originally intended as an escape hatch. The main door to the hide was beneath the staircase which now leads to the administrator's flat. The provision of two approaches to a hide, a device which afforded a priest some chance of escape should pursuivants uncover his whereabouts, is another feature of Owen's work. The secret space at Oxburgh, brilliantly concealed beneath a pivoting panel of tiles, was provided with a seat and even a small opening into the King's Room through which, it has been suggested, drinks could be discreetly funnelled into the hide. By this means an occupant could be refreshed during a prolonged spell of incarceration. The security of the hide is vouched for by the fact that Oxburgh was twice raided by pursuivants, who left empty-handed on each occasion.

Though we cannot be certain, Owen was probably also responsible for the hides at Baddesley Clinton in Warwickshire, another delightful moated manor house now in the care of the National Trust. As with the hide at Scotney Castle, we have been left with a written account of a priest hole in action. The tale is vigorously, if subjectively, related in the autobiography of Father Gerard. He does not mention the scene of the adventure by name, but we can be sure from the detail he provides that it was Baddesley Clinton, then tenanted from the Catholic Henry Ferrers by two recusant sisters of the Vaux family, Miss Anne Vaux and Mrs Eleanor Brooksby.

In mid-October 1591 the house was chosen by the Jesuits as the venue for one of the conferences which they held twice a year to review progress and foster spiritual awareness. Before the meeting took place a suspicious pursuivant named Hodgkins arrived at the door. Angry at having been kept waiting while incriminating evidence was disposed of, he announced that he would shortly return with some helpers and pull the place apart.

Catholic accounts of the behaviour of pursuivants such as
Hodgkins are understandably critical. No doubt this is due
in some degree to straightforward snobbery: many priests
came from well-to-do families and they resented being
harassed in the homes of the gentry by their social
inferiors. It is also clear, however, that the office of
pursuivant tended to attract an unpleasant, bullying sort
of character, prepared to stoop to any devious or rough
tactic to get his hands on the substantial reward offered by
the government for the successful arrest of a priest.

Anxious that the uncouth Hodgkins might reappear at
any moment, a number of priests and laymen left the
house as soon as the business had been completed. At
about five o' clock the next morning, Gerard reports, 'I
was making my meditation, Father Southwell was
beginning Mass and the rest were at prayer, when
suddenly I heard a great uproar outside the main door.
Then I heard a voice shouting and swearing ...' Hodgkins
had returned.

There were four pursuivants at the door, all armed with
swords and demanding to be let in at once. The Vaux
servants had been prepared for such an eventuality, and
while the priests scuttled away into their hiding place ('a
very cleverly built sort of cave') with their massing stuff, a
number of excuses was used to delay the entry of the
Hodgkins gang. There was even time to turn the
matresses of the priests' beds, so that the warm sides
faced downwards.

'At last these leopards were let in. They tore madly
through the whole house, searched everywhere, pried
with candles into the darkest corner. They took four hours
over the work but fortunately they chanced on nothing.'
The search was a good example of how not to catch a
recusant priest. The household were permitted to remain
in the building; the vital element of surprise had been lost
by Hodgkins' warning and the delay at the gate; there was
clearly nothing systematic about the hunt, no measuring
or comparing of the inside with the outside of the house;
and the whole operation was finished much too quickly.
As we have already seen, the best chance of driving a

priest from his secret lair was to starve him out. Hodgkins' rapid and furious search was an insult to the ingenuity of Nicholas Owen, who was probably responsible for the 'sort of cave' at Baddesley Clinton.

The National Trust guidebook speaks of three hides at Baddesley Clinton. Hodgetts recognizes only two. The confusion arises from the fact that beneath the walls of the house there runs a long medieval drain which at one time was divided into two separate hiding places. The section used at the time of the Hodgkins search lies beneath the southern corner of the building. It was once approached down an old latrine shaft in the sacristy, though it is now viewed through a glass window in the kitchen. On the opposite side of the house another part of the underground priest hole can be seen in a corner of the Moat Room. Its original entrance was through the fireplace in the Great Parlour. The second or third hide, probably dating from the 1580s, is in the roof above the front bedroom. The details of the hides are ultimately immaterial. What the visitor is given at Baddesley Clinton is a wonderful opportunity to let the imagination recreate one of the more fascinating episodes in Tudor history.

Throughout the reign of Elizabeth I Lancashire harboured more Roman Catholics than most other parts of the kingdom. Four delightful houses, each containing priest holes, bear witness to the survival of the old faith in this conservative northern county. Towneley Hall, managed by Burnley Borough Council, Lancashire, has been extensively rebuilt since the sixteenth century and today it is worth visiting more as an art gallery than as an introduction to recusant history. Nevertheless, the Hall is unique in that we have a written record of the hides which it once contained. There were nine in all, though only one survives. It is at the head of the eighteenth-century cantilever staircase, between the ceiling of the parlour and the servants' bedroom. The hidey hole occupies about 20 square metres, sufficient for a whole army of recusants. It has been suggested that this secret hiding place remained when others were removed in case it might be needed by members of the Towneley family with Jacobite sympathies.

Speke Hall in Liverpool (National Trust) and Samlesbury Hall (Samlesbury Hall Trust) are outstanding examples of timber-framed black-and-white houses for which Britain is famous. In the later sixteenth century Speke was owned by the Catholic Edward Norris, who made extensive alterations to the building in 1598. It is not surprising, therefore, to find hides in the part of the building which was constructed at that time. One is behind the panelling in the Green Room, the other is entered from a trapdoor in the attics above the Tapestry Room. Edward Norris was a cautious man, and although the authorities knew that Speke was used for harbouring recusant priests, there are no dramatic stories connected with the hides. Edward's successor at Speke, Sir William Norris, was far less careful about concealing his faith, and when he died in 1651 he had brought the family estates to the verge of bankruptcy.

Samlesbury was also watched closely by the Elizabethan authorities. Its owner, Sir John Southworth, was a celebrated recusant whose career offers a good example of the relatively lenient and sporadic enforcement of the potentially harsh penalties against law-abiding Catholics. He was imprisoned twice, but set free when he promised to move from Lancashire to London. He was not re-arrested when he returned to Samlesbury in 1586. By October of the next year the Privy Council noted that the arrears of his recusancy fines totalled £1,060, an enormous sum not surprisingly unpaid since the £240 per annum which open adherence to the Catholic faith cost amounted to more than the whole of the annual income from the Samlesbury estates. Sir John had little choice but to back down and attend Anglican services. The government were delighted at such a notable conversion, and in 1592 the last of Sir John's debts were remitted after no less a person than the Archbishop of Canterbury had vouched for the sincerity of the ex-papist's new faith.

The change of heart was shortlived. In 1592 the Council sent the following command to a local JP, Richard Brereton:

Next Tuesday, an hour before dawn, be at the house of Sir John Southworth with a number of trusty servants. Make a most careful search of the building, examining all rooms, lofts, studies and cellars, keeping an eye open for secret and suspicious places. Try to discover any Jesuit or seminary priests who may be hidden there. Also be on the look out for arms and any suspicious papers or pamphlets.

(cited in Alistair C. Hodge, Samlesbury:
A Short History, 1986).

The raid was made on 21 November. It revealed no suspected persons, but it did turn up 'a gown without a pocket' and some Catholic literature. It also revealed 'a secret vault over the dining chamber'. The Hall has subsequently been extensively altered, but this hide is usually considered to be the space in the roof of the Great Hall, near the Minstrels' Gallery.

Chingle Hall, the oldest brick building in Britain and also said to be the most haunted house in the country, was one of the most successful Catholic centres in Lancashire. It never appeared on Lord Burghley's map of suspected places, although the Catholic Singleton family were forced by recusancy fines to sell the property in 1600. The building's six hides, three for priests and the others for documents, are said to have been designed by Nicholas Owen in about 1600. The mansion is particularly rewarding to visit because it is a private home and not merely a tourist trap. Its medley of false beams and windows, chimney hide and rediscovered chapel, provide the twentieth-century pursuivant with a perfect setting in which to test his or her skills as a hide hunter.

The delightful Oxfordshire mansion of Stonor is another house which has been closely associated with Roman Catholicism over the centuries. In 1581 it served as the headquarters for Edmund Campion and Robert Parsons, the first Jesuit missionary priests to be sent to England during the reign of Elizabeth I. The Catholic tract *Ten Reasons* was printed here, probably on a secret press housed in a small room above the fourteenth-century hall. The press and other incriminating Catholic material were found at Stonor when government officers searched the house in August 1581. The house also possesses a vast hide in the roof, a cunningly contrived entrance to which was uncovered in the Little Attic bedroom in 1964.

The best-known priest hole in Wales is at Plas Mawr in Gwynedd. The hide is an early one, situated on the first floor in a chimney between the Reception Room and the haunted Lantern Room. Before visiting the house, those with an interest in the paranormal may care to read the story connected with this chamber in Bernard Wood's *Secret Britain*.

The priest hole at Dalemain, Cumbria, was discovered in the housekeeper's room in the middle of the last century. It was entered up the kitchen fireplace, and when the priest was safely ensconced within it a fire was lit below to deter prying pursuivants. Today there is access to the hide through the housekeeper's store cupboard.

Rainthorpe Hall in Norfolk has a priest hole beside a chimney in the master bedroom. At one time the flue was fitted with iron rungs leading from the fireplace in the Great Hall below, though it is uncertain whether these were for the convenience of fugitive priests or chimney sweeps. The hole has now been converted into a hanging cupboard. Its presence was made startlingly obvious by the mother of the present owner of the Hall, who embarked on the task of staining the panelling in the room but changed her mind after completing only the door to the hide. Lord Burghley would undoubtably have approved of her action.

Several other houses equipped with secret hiding places for priests are dealt with in connection with the 1605 Gunpowder Plot (see Chapter 4), but that still leaves numerous others. There is an Owen hide at Braddocks in Essex, a building which for several years acted as a focus for recusants in the area. The house was the subject of a successful pursuivant raid in 1592 which uncovered a considerable cache of arms and an elderly priest named Richard Jackson, who had been discreetly ministering to the faithful since the reign of Queen Mary I. Together with important correspondence and popish regalia the priest was discovered in an inadequate hide, which was why Owen was brought in a short while later to improve the security arrangements at Braddocks. He built the hide out of the solid brickwork beneath the chapel, and prepared for lengthy occupation by the provision of a seat and even a small latrine. There is a similar *de luxe* hide by Owen at Sawston Hall, Cambridgeshire. It is brilliantly concealed and compares most favourably with two earlier hidey holes in the same building.

Ripley Castle in North Yorkshire, the home of Sir Thomas and Lady Ingilby, has a fine early priest hole in the delightful panelled room known as the Knight's Chamber. The hole was discovered in 1964 when the room was being treated for woodworm and dry rot. No one knows for how long it had remained closed. It was probably built in 1584 for the priest Francis Ingilby, who was executed at York two years later. The hide was found to contain an unusual feature: it had a blackout attached to the inside of the door to prevent the light of an occupant's candle being visible through the cracks in the woodwork when the chamber outside was in darkness. Other priest holes exist at Cavendish Manor in Suffolk, and at Rufford Old Hall and Hoghton Tower, both in Lancashire; all are open to the public. There is even a hideaway believed to be a priest hole in the Mermaid Inn in Rye, Sussex.

Many houses have unexplained secret spaces which may at one time have served as hiding holes for priests. One of the most interesting is at Filching Manor, East Sussex, a building already noticed for its tunnel. In the right-hand corner of the hall the panelling swings forward to reveal a cupboard in a converted latrine shaft that once led from the first floor to the basement. The space has at some time been fitted with a floor and ancient hinges indicate that the present door replaces a much older one. The history of Filching is only now being assembled, but there is every probability that the cavity behind the woodwork was originally created to provide a secure hide for recusants. The manor also has a large unexplained space behind the wall of a private bedroom on the first floor, where the older part of the building adjoins a later extension. The present owner of the property intends to open up the cavity one day, and it will be interesting to see what he finds.

Among other houses with mysterious secret cavities are

Melford Hall in Suffolk, Newark Park in Gloucestershire, Levens Hall in Cumbria, Newick Park and Parham, both in Sussex, and Dunster Castle in Somerset. More frustrating, however, are the several houses which are known to have priest holes but which do not make them part of their tourist itinerary. Such places include the remarkable half-timbered Gawsworth Hall in Cheshire and the magnificent Elizabethan mansion of Burton Constable Hall in Humberside. Other houses which certainly merit a visit but which do not display their priest holes to the general public include Ludford House in Shropshire, Mapledurham in Berkshire and Meols Hall on Merseyside.

Perhaps we should conclude with a reference to Leighton Hall in Lancashire, which must surely be just about the only ancient Catholic mansion in that county which does not boast of a single hide, passage or tunnel. The only remotely secret feature is the burial ground where Catholics were quietly laid to rest with the rites of their outlawed Church. When Catholic emancipation came the bodies were dug up and reburied in the village churchyard. Today nothing will grow on the ancient burial site, in spite of it being in the middle of a wood. And the priests? 'I think that we were so far away from anywhere', writes Mrs Reynolds, one of the present owners of the house, 'that if there was any hint of danger the priest just rushed off into the woods!' Even Nicholas Owen could not compete with nature when it came to building the best hides.

4   Plots and Persecutions

After we had been in the hole seven days and seven nights and some odd hours, every man may well think we were well wearied, and so indeed it was ... When we came forth, we appeared like two ghosts.

Father Henry Garnet, 1606

It is estimated that when Queen Elizabeth died in 1603 about 40,000 of her subjects still adhered to the Roman Catholic faith. They were served by some 300 priests, who were divided almost equally between the seculars and those in regular orders. The former were the equivalent of parish priests, while the latter were mostly Jesuits, though the Benedictines were formally established in England in 1618. Only nineteen priests were executed during the reign of James I and VI (1603–25), but the missionaries' lot continued to be a tough one. Not surprisingly, therefore, we find recusant families continuing to use existing hides and, on occasion, to build new ones in which to shelter their clerical protégés.

At Turton Tower in Lancashire, for example, a sixteenth-century doorway from the chapel into the drawing room is disguised as a cupboard. The deceit was included in an inventory of the house made in 1651, which listed the chapel as a bedroom, so the alteration must have been made at some time in the first half of the seventeenth century to conceal the presence of the chapel. There was another secret chapel at Torre Abbey, Devon. Built as late as 1662 by the Catholic Cary family, it was hidden above

above the roof of the dining room. After the Catholic Relief Act of 1778 the Carys were permitted to worship openly and moved into a purpose-built chapel in the Great Hall of the Abbey. They then redesigned their dining room, giving it a vaulted ceiling and so destroying the old secret chapel above it. The vestry and the stairs which led to the chapel can still be seen, though they are not on view to the public. The last record of the construction of an actual priest hole pertains to that at Capheaton in Northumberland. The house is not generally open to visitors, though the grounds may be visited by appointment. The so-called 'secret room' at Little Moreton Hall in Cheshire is a seventeenth-century construction, but all available evidence suggests that it was used as servants' quarters and not as a hiding place. Nevertheless, the Hall is a delight to visit as it is one of the finest timber-framed moated manor houses in the country and has some splendid sixteenth-century wall paintings.

There are one or two priest holes dating from earlier in the seventeenth century. Michael Hodgetts makes a good case for including among these the hide at Carlton Towers on Humberside, previously reckoned to be a Victorian reconstruction (see Chapter 9). The original house was begun in 1614. Another hide which may date from about this time is to be found within Lord William's Tower in the rugged border fortress of Naworth Castle, Cumbria. The priest hole at Treowen Court (Gwent) is also very likely to be a seventeenth-century construction, put in at the same time as the Jacobean staircase. The headquarters of John Salisbury, the Jesuit superior in Wales for much of the reign of James I, was at Raglan Castle, also in Gwent. The castle has no specific priest hole, but during the outbursts of anti-papal feeling which flared up from time to time Salisbury and his co-religionists may well have secreted themselves in the windowless strong room of the Yellow Tower.

The English Roman Catholic community had some reason for optimism when Elizabeth was replaced on the throne by an intellectual Scotsman with a declared propensity for toleration and peace. King James accepted the spiritual authority of the papacy and said that he had no wish to persecute Roman Catholics 'that will be quiet and give but an outward obedience to the law'. His wife, Anne of Denmark, had converted to Catholicism in the 1590s, providing a further reason for James' declaration that 'I will never allow in my conscience that the blood of any man shall be shed for diversity of opinion in religion'. In 1604, while ordering that all Jesuits and seminary priests leave the kingdom, he relaxed the penal laws against Catholics. The result of the new policy was unfortunate, but predictable. Within a short time contemporaries were complaining that papists 'lived in jollity' compared with former times, and 'have grown mightily in number, courage and influence'. This is clearly an exaggeration. But it was not reality so much as what men believed to be happening that mattered. James was ahead of his time. The phobia of Catholicism would not evaporate at the will of an alien monarch and, prompted by parliamentary opposition, within a short time James was obliged to stiffen his policies towards the Catholics in order to maintain the goodwill of the majority of his subjects.

Moreover, even James' toleration was limited. He distinguished between loyal Catholic subjects and missionary priests. He was particularly antipathetic towards the Jesuits, those 'venomous wasps and firebrands of sedition' who owed allegiance directly to the papacy and who spearheaded the international Counter-Reformation. The problem with the king's separation of Roman Catholic beliefs from politics was that the Pope claimed the right to temporal as well as spiritual power. He had, after all, theoretically deposed Elizabeth and could still do the same to her successors. It was not realistic, James' critics pointed out, to believe that a true Catholic could owe equal allegiance to both king and Pope. And it was not long before a fanatical minority of the king's subjects seemed to prove them right.

The origin of the celebrated 1605 Gunpowder Plot lay in the terms of the peace treaty which James made with

Spain in 1604. English Catholics had long hoped that when an agreement was eventually made with Spain it would include a clause granting them full toleration. To their intense disappointment, no such agreement was reached. Most Catholics took the unhappy news in their stride and looked forward to an easing of their lot under the new king now that the military threat from Spain was removed. But a tiny and unrepresentative band of young hotheads thought otherwise. They saw the Treaty of London as the final confirmation that the English government could not be moved by negotiation. They believed the only course now open to them was force.

The aim of the plotters was to blow up a good part of the Palace of Westminster on the day when Parliament was being opened by the king. They hoped that the explosion would remove the king, Henry Prince of Wales, the Privy Council and many members of both the Lords and Commons. In the resultant confusion they planned to lead a rising in the Midlands, take over the government and place one of James' children, either Prince Charles or Princess Elizabeth, on the throne. The original plotters were led by Robert Catesby, who had backed the abortive rebellion of the Earl of Essex in 1601. (The hide at the Manor House at Chenies in Hertfordshire was probably constructed by the third Earl of Bedford prior to his setting out to take part in this foolish venture.) Catesby was joined by Thomas, Robert and John Winter (or Wintour), Thomas Perry, Guy Fawkes and two of his old schoolmates, John and Christopher Wright. In the summer of 1605 Father Henry Garnet and one or two other Jesuit priests got wind of what was planned. The proposed *coup* put them in a difficult position. Should it fail, which was most likely, their cause would be set back many years and their lives would be in mortal danger. On the other hand, if the operation were to succeed they would not wish to be known as men who had counselled against it. Their quandary was all the more taxing as they had come to hear of the plot through the religious confessions of the conspirators. They therefore urged them to be cautious. In the aftermath of the discovery of the plot the government was quick to claim that the Jesuits had masterminded the conspiracy. The reaction was understandable, but unfounded. There have even been those who have argued that the whole idea of a plot was concocted by Robert Cecil (Lord Salisbury) to discredit the Catholics. Garnet's trial in 1606, involving a clash between the sanctity of the confession and national security, attracted a great deal of attention, both at home and abroad. Even King James attended daily in secret. The priest was eventually found guilty of treason, although no modern court would have reached such a verdict.

The story of the plot is well known. It began with the excavation of one of Britain's most renowned secret tunnels, from the cellar of a house nearby to the vaults beneath the House of Lords. The passage is as elusive as it is famous. There are no records of anyone seeing it after 1605, and what traces there might have been vanished when the Houses of Parliament were destroyed by fire in the nineteenth century. As it turned out, the tunnel was never used, for in March 1605 the conspirators managed to hire a cellar adjacent to those of the Lords. From there it was simple enough to knock a doorway through and fill the palace vault with twenty barrels of gunpowder, covered with iron bars to increase the destructive power of the blast. The dump was then concealed beneath piles of faggots.

The desperate scheme was revealed when the original circle of plotters was increased to include Francis Tresham, who sent an anonymous letter to Lord Monteagle warning him not to attend the ceremony on 5 November. He passed the letter to Lord Salisbury, who in turn showed it to the king. Two separate search parties were arranged. On 4 November the gunpowder was discovered and Guy Fawkes was arrested. Over the next few months most of the conspirators and a number of Catholic priests were rounded up, tortured and executed. Among their number was Nicholas Owen, the master hide-builder, who died when 'his bowels gushed out' under torture in the Tower (from *John Gerard: The Autobiography of an Elizabethan*, ed. Philip Caraman, 1986).

Several houses with secret hiding places are associated, directly and indirectly, with the Gunpowder Plot. The Winter brothers lived at Huddington Court (Hereford and Worcester), a house which may at present be visited by prior arrangement with its owner, Professor Hugh Edmondson. It was here that a number of thwarted conspirators gathered on 7 November to hear mass said by the house's resident Jesuit priest, Father Nicholas Hart. The service took place in a secret roof chapel which can still be seen above the Great Chamber. After the service all Catholic paraphenalia, including a cross, a chalice and many books, were hidden in a hole in the wall. This secret depository can no longer be identified, though the house does boast two fine priest holes which were almost certainly the work of Nicholas Owen. The larger of the two, occupying an enormous 24 cubic metres of space, is on the same floor as the chapel and is entered through a door camouflaged to appear like sections of lath-and-plaster on either side of a wooden joist. The second hide leads from the wainscot of the chapel itself. The presence of an inner hide within the outer one, an emergency exit and carefully disguised doors are all hallmarks of Owen's work.

Coughton Court in Warwickshire has been the home of the Throckmorton family since 1409. The Throckmortons were related to the de Vaux family and several of the Gunpowder Plot conspirators, notably the Treshams and Catesby. Edward Throckmorton died while training at the English College in Rome in 1582. Francis Throckmorton had been executed in 1584 for conspiring to overthrow Queen Elizabeth with the aid of Catholic forces from the continent and place Mary Queen of Scots on the throne. It has been suggested that the Court was an important centre for the celebration of mass from the time of Queen Mary onwards. It is hardly surprising, therefore, to find the house featuring in this story of treason and plot.

The owner of Coughton Court, Thomas Throckmorton, had decided to leave for the continent at the time the Gunpowder Plot was hatched. It is possible that he had heard what was afoot and, having lost one member of the family in an unsuccessful conspiracy twenty years before, had decided that on this occasion discretion was the better part of valour. His caution was fully justified. His house was lent to Sir Everard Digby, who was given the task of commanding the Warwickshire rebels in the rising which was to follow the debacle at Westminster. Sir Everard and his household moved to Coughton at the end of October. Among their number were Lady Digby, Garnet and Owen. They took with them a cartload of weapons and ammunition. On 6 November a messenger arrived at Coughton bearing a letter which told of the failure of the *coup*. 'We [are] all utterly undone!' (from *John Gerard*) muttered Garnet when he heard the news. Lady Digby became hysterical, and Garnet, accompanied by his loyal servant Owen, decided to stay on at Coughton to comfort her. They remained in hiding until 4 December, during which time Garnet wrote to the Privy Council professing his innocence.

In Tudor and Stuart times Coughton was a square house built around a courtyard. Unfortunately the fourth side of the building, which held the major chapel, was pulled down in 1720. It is likely that one or two Owen hides were destroyed in the demolition. We are left with a small secret chapel in the gatehouse and three priest holes of uncertain date. The largest was probably built during the 1580s. It is on two floors beneath a privy in the turret off the Tower Room. Though it comprises the relatively sophisticated concept of a hide beneath a hide, the external location of the hiding place made it easy to find for any experienced pursuivant – 3 metres of windowless tower take some explaining away. A second hide, on the ground floor, was later converted into a wine cellar and we have no idea how it appeared in Owen's time. A third hide, which also may have featured an inner sanctum, is to be found near the dining room, but it too has been considerably altered over the centuries.

Sir Francis Tresham, the father of the plotter Francis, lived at Rushton Hall in Northamptonshire. The house has no hides, but in 1823 a valuable collection of ancient papers was discovered above a door lintel. They had been hidden there by Francis Tresham at the time of the Plot.

There is an Owen hide at Thrumpton Hall, Notting-hamshire, the home of the Powdrell family who were involved on the fringes of the 1605 conspiracy. Father Garnet is supposed to have sheltered at Thrumpton for a while. As far as accessible architectural evidence is con-cerned, the story of the Gunpowder Plot ends here. Apart from the ghastly epilogue in the torture chamber of the Tower and on the scaffold, the last scene of the eventful tragedy took place at Hindlip Hall, a house which was demolished in 1814. By all accounts it contained the finest collection of hides and priest holes in the country.

Owen and Garnet moved to Hindlip in early December. They were joined by Father Oldcorne, the priest who regularly served the Hall. Early in 1606 the conspirator Humphrey Lyttelton revealed their whereabouts to the government, and on 20 January Hindlip was surrounded by a large force of armed men. The most famous search of all began an hour or so later. Lord Treasurer Robert Cecil clearly knew Hindlip well, for he sent Sir Henry Bromley, the Sheriff of Worcestershire and the man responsible for the search, a detailed letter of instructions. Perhaps he did not trust Sir Henry's intelligence or efficiency, for he knew that the man had searched the house in 1598 and failed to find Father Oldcorne. Cecil's command ran:

> In the search, first observe the parlour where they dine and sup; in the east part of that parlour it is conceived there is some vault; which to discover you must take care to draw down the wainscot, whereby the entry to the vault may be discovered. And the lower parts of the house must be tried with a broach, by putting same into the ground a foot or two to try whether there be some timber, which if there be, there must be some vault underneath it. For the upper rooms, you must observe whether they be more in breadth than the lower rooms, and look in the places the rooms be enlarged; by pulling up some boards you may discover some vaults.
>
> (*John Gerard: A Narrative of the Gunpowder Plot*, Ed. John Morris, 1872)

In his *Secret Passages and Hiding-Places* Jeremy Errand says that Hindlip had an escape tunnel which was still serviceable in the 1970s. It is more likely, however, that this was a large drain. It is odd, if there had been a secret means of egress, that the trapped priests did not use it when Sir Henry Bromley's men were battering down Hindlip's gates in 1606.

The search party did as they had been bidden by the government. For several days, however, all that they came across were some scholarly papers, clothing and suspiciously warm bedding, and other 'Popish trash' hidden beneath the floorboards. At the end of the third day Sir Henry went home, leaving his brother to continue the hunt. We now know that the sherrif had made one of the fundamental errors of priest hunting: he had failed to clear all members of the household from the premises being searched. Dorothy Habington, the mistress of the household, was able to supply the priests with hot drinks fed down a quill into their hide from her bedroom. It seems as if she was unable to help Owen and a fellow servant in this manner, however, and on the fourth day they could stand their captivity no longer. Cramped, frozen and starving (they had taken but a single apple with them into their hide), they decided to try what we might call the 'Scotney trick' of giving themselves up and pretending that they were the only people secreted in the building. The pursuivants were looking for two priests, so there was a chance that the servants' ruse might have worked. In fact it had the opposite effect. The two men had hoped to slip away unobserved from the Long Gallery in which their hide lay, but two guards saw them before they had taken a few steps, and within minutes the panelling of the Gallery was being hacked to pieces.

It was a further four days before Garnet and Oldcorne were found in their hide. The conditions of their detention had become unendurable. Not only were the men cramped and cold but they suffered dreadfully from the stuffy air of the place and from the fact that it contained no adequate lavatory. There was some form of crude urinal, which must have been filled to overflowing after all Mrs

Habington's drinks, but there was no bucket for solid waste. Rather than foul their hide, the priests engaged on a self-imposed eight-day bout of constipation. The searchers realized that this was probably a problem for their hidden quarry and, believing that they would have to make a clandestine nocturnal visit to the privy, they set a trap there. This involved taking up one of the boards covering the pit, so that in the darkness an unwary visitor would fall through the floor into the sewage below. As soon as he had been captured, the desperate Father Garnet asked to be allowed to go to the privy, which is how he discovered the stratagem which had been arranged there. Fortunately it was daylight when he made the visit, so he emerged still clean and much relieved a short while later.

No fewer than eleven hiding places were uncovered at Hindlip, all but one of which seem to have been rendered useless by the pursuivants. Thomas Habington, who owned the house, was sentenced to death but later reprieved on condition that he remained within the boundaries of Worcestershire for the remainder of his life. This he was only too pleased to do.

The immediate effect of the Gunpowder Plot was to make life very hard for the Catholic community. In 1606 the Penal Laws were made much tougher: papists were banned from public office, they were not permitted to come into or near London, they could not practise law, and they were made liable to confiscation of two-thirds of their lands rather than the £20 per month fine imposed by Elizabethan legislation. Toughest of all was the Oath of Allegiance, drawn up personally by the king, which all Catholics had to swear. Its aim (cited in Roger Lockyer's *The Early Stuarts*, 1989) was to distinguish between traitors and others who 'although they were otherwise popishly affected, yet retained in their hearts the print of their natural duty to their sovreign'. The final clause of the oath presented Catholics with the greatest problem, for it asked them to accept that the Pope's right to excommunicate princes was 'impious and heretical'. It also insisted on their swearing that: 'neither the Pope nor any person whatsoever hath power to absolve me of this oath or any part thereof'. Since this was a direct challenge to his authority, the pontiff was swift to condemn the oath. Nevertheless, many Catholics took it, including a good number of priests, and although James had failed in his aim of securing the sworn loyalty of all his popish subjects, tension steadily declined as the reign wore on.

By 1640 there were about 60,000 Catholics in the country; 750 of these were priests, of whom about 400 were Jesuits. This is said to have been the greatest number in post-Reformation England before the mid-nineteenth century. Three Catholic priests were executed in the 1620s, none in the 1630s. The total number of Catholics also belies their influence. They may have been a mere 1 per cent of the population, but they comprised 20 per cent of the peerage in 1642, and many of them held high office.

It would be wrong to assume from this that there was widespread toleration of Roman Catholics by ordinary men and women, or that persecution declined along some steady curve. As late as the nineteenth century anti-Catholic riots could flare up at any moment. (Indeed, as the tragic situation in Northern Ireland bears witness, in some regions the old animosities have still not died out.) At times of tension and war in the seventeenth century, when popular resentment demanded a search for scapegoats, recusant families still found it prudent to clean out their priest holes in case it proved necessary to shelter some fugitive father. James II's tactlessly expounded Catholicism cost him his throne, and in 1679–80 the Popish Plot scare saw a particularly nasty outbreak of irrational anti-Catholic feeling.

There was in fact no Popish Plot. The whole thing was the fabrication of two scurrilous rogues, Titus Oates and Israel Tonge. But they launched their story on a frightened populace, and when their accusations were given plausibility by one or two fortuitous discoveries, public disquiet rose rapidly to a storm of hatred for Catholics. Nine Jesuits were executed, twelve died in prison and another three perished as a direct result of the Plot. Francis Bruning and Charles Pritchard, for example, were chased for eighteen months until they dropped dead from sheer exhaustion. Six other priests were executed, at least three died in prison, and one was detained in Bedlam as a lunatic. Several more, both Jesuits and others, were held in prison for many years. Though the persecution was hap- hazard, it was terrifying enough for the priests who suf- fered it. 'Sweet Jesus grant us patience in all our adversity', wrote one man who found himself 'daily interrupted by frequent alarms and breaking up of our quarters, enough to daunt an old soldier and make such novices as myself sneak into lurking holes'. (From J.P. Kenyon, *The Popish Plot*, 1974).

It is not easy to find reference to specific 'lurking' holes used by Catholic priests at this time. We may safely assume, however, that they were those which had been in service, on and off, since the time of Elizabeth. We know that the hides at Boscobel, for example, one of which had served Charles II so well in 1651 (see Chapter 5), were at this time once more used to conceal priests. In 1600 Chingle Hall (see page 69) had been acquired by the Catholic Wall family. John Wall, who was born in 1620, became a Franciscan, working as a missionary in the Midlands before he was arrested in 1679 and executed. His head is supposed to have been rescued by some friends and taken to Douai. From here it found its way to the house of the Poor Clares at Aire, where it remained a revered relic until the French Revol- ution. It was then brought back to England until in 1815 conditions on the continent were felt safe enough for its re-export. Twenty-one years later the order came that it should be restored to the country upon which its living eyes had gazed a century and a half previously. But the sister charged with the mission balked at her grisly task, and buried the head in the convent garden. It then disappeared. According to legend it had been smuggled into England and concealed somewhere in Chingle Hall, perhaps in a for- gotten hide which John Wall himself had explored as a child. It is reasonable to assume that the several priest holes in Wall's birthplace also served as a safe refuge for Catholic priests during the time of the Popish Plot scare.

It is interesting to note the change which had come over

the country in the century between the Spanish Armada and the Popish Plot. In the 1580s and 90s it was the government which had led the hunt for Popish priests. A century later most ministers, and certainly Charles II himself, remained sceptical about the whole episode. The attacks on the Catholics were instigated by pressure from some MPs and other vocal community leaders, not from the government. The degree of action taken depended entirely upon local justices, so in many counties the Catholic community survived unscathed. In some instances the Plot was used to settle personal vendettas. There is a story of one Protestant landowner ordering the arrest of a Catholic priest merely because the man had refused to sanction the marriage of the gentleman's son to a Catholic heiress. The unfortunate victim was later executed, one of the last priests to suffer such a fate for his religion.

Although the experiment of a Roman Catholic monarch failed in 1688, the plot marked the end of sustained outbursts of anti-Catholic violence. The severe Penal Laws remained on the statute book for a long time to come and were added to when Catholics were ordered to pay double Land Tax in 1692, but the execution of Oliver Plunkett on 1 July 1681 brought a cruel tradition to an end. Scorned and impoverished though they might be, by the end of the century Roman Catholic priests rarely went about their duties in fear for their lives. Priest holes had finally become obsolete.

The story of the persecution of Protestant nonconformists leaves no physical evidence comparable to the priest holes of the recusants. The Lollard followers of John Wycliffe were hunted down in the fifteenth century, but none of their hides remain. Henry VIII dealt firmly with both Protestants and Papists who expressed dissatisfaction with his Anglo-Catholic Church of England. No doubt many hid to escape arrest, as did Protestant opponents of his daughters Mary and Elizabeth, though no hiding place used by them is on view today. The same situation pertains to seventeenth-century England, when puritans whose teaching seemed to threaten both Church and state were on occasion rounded up. It is only in Scotland that persecution of a puritan minority was carried out systematically and ruthlessly.

The Scots' National Covenant began as a protest against the attempts of Charles I and Archbishop William Laud to impose an Anglican style of Church on the northern king- dom. Within a year or so royal authority in Scotland was at best precarious and the Presbyterian Covenanters dictated the form and style of the Scottish Church. With the return of Charles II and episcopal Church government in 1660, however, the more earnest Covenanters, known as Protes- ters or Conventiclers, found themselves out of favour. For the next thirty years the authorities played a cat-and-mouse game with them, alternating a policy of leniency with one of severe repression, particularly after 1679.

Anyone touring south-west Scotland today will be sure to come across the many monuments to the dour but brave men and women who persisted with their religious prac- tices in the face of rigorous persecution. More often than not they met in private houses or in the open air, favouring small mossy glens or woods which could be closely guarded. At Wigtown there is a post marking the spot where two women Covenanters were tied to stakes at the mouth of the River Bladnoch and left to drown in the rising tide. The monument at Windyhill behind the town comme- morates all those martyred for their adherence to the Cove- nant. But no one now can point with certainty to the many places where they conducted their secret services, or where they took refuge from the soldiers of John Graham of Claverhouse during what became known as the 'killing time'. In Loudoun churchyard lies the grave of John Law, who perished along with many of his fellow Covenanters when dragoons came across a conventicle being held at Little Blackwood. James White is remembered in nearby Fenwick churchyard. He was shot when soldiers broke up a clandestine meeting which he was conducting. Legend says that the executioners then cut off his head and used it as a football. The region is thick with such bitter stories. Clearly Protestants could be just as cruel to each other as they were to their Roman Catholic contemporaries.

5 Cavaliers on the Run

I knew that they had hiding holes for priests that I thought
I might make use of in case of need …

Charles II

For years one of the most powerful and popular images of
the Civil War (1642–5) was that created by William
Frederick Yeames' celebrated Victorian painting *And When
Did You Last See Your Father?*. Though obviously a romantic
recreation, the picture is powerfully evocative of the sort
of scene which must have occurred in several great houses
during 1644 and 1645, as all over the country the
Parliamentary armies began to get the upper hand and
Cavalier officers were forced to go into hiding.

There is little evidence of secret hidey holes or tunnels
being constructed specifically for use in the war. In the
farmhouse wing of Bickleigh Castle in Devon there is a
cavity beside the chimney on the first floor. Since the
house was built in *c*.1650–60, replacing the medieval
fortifications destroyed by General Fairfax, the small
rectangular opening may have been included specifically
as a hide for use by members of the royalist Carew family.
On the other hand, it could equally well have been
designed as a priest hole.

Hides and passages already in existence were certainly
employed during the war, as we have seen at Tiverton
(page 27) and Wardour (page 29). The great drain at
Kirby Hall in Northamptonshire, rediscovered as recently
as 1987, may have served as an escape route for the

Royalist Hatton family. Secret places of concealment built for recusants were put to a new use at, among other places, Boscobel, Heale, Moseley Old Hall, Ripley Castle and Chastleton. The hide at Ripley may quite possibly have been where the royalist Sir William Ingilby spent the night of 2–3 July 1644 after the defeat of Prince Rupert's army at Marston Moor. Sir William had every reason to make himself scarce, for no less a person than Oliver Cromwell had chosen the ground floor library of Ripley Castle as a place to rest after the fight.

Seven years later a similar scene is reported to have been enacted at Chastleton House in Oxfordshire. Following the defeat of Charles II at the Battle of Worcester on 3 September 1651, scores of Royalists fled from the field, pursued by the Parliamentary cavalry. Captain Arthur Jones rode home to Chastleton House in Oxfordshire as quickly as his horse would carry him, arriving only minutes before a troop of Ironsides. Having shut her husband in a secret chamber off the main bedroom, Sarah Jones then went downstairs to open the door to the Roundheads. Noticing an exhausted horse standing in the stables, they were certain that they had cornered their prey and demanded to search the house. Sarah did not object to the soldiers' request. Indeed, she appeared to afford them every assistance, even offering to guide them round the property herself.

It was past midnight by the time this fruitless exercise was completed, and the men were exhausted after their long and gruelling day. In the circumstances, therefore, they decided to spend the night at Chastleton, selecting as their dormitory the most comfortable accommodation – the house's main bed chamber. Nothing daunted, Mrs Jones provided them with plentiful food and drink (laced, according to some accounts, with opium taken from the family medicine chest), and bade them a gracious goodnight.

An hour later Sarah crept back to the bedroom to find the soldiers fast asleep, scattered about the floor as if they had been shot, and snoring like oxen. Carefully, she tiptoed to the concealed door, released her husband, and led him to the stables. Here he selected the freshest looking of his enemies' horses, and rode off into the night. By the time the search party came to their senses the next morning, unbeknown to them their quarry was miles away. After further sampling of Mrs Jones' hospitality at breakfast, they apologized for the inconvenience they had caused and went to prepare their mounts. The missing horse took some explaining, but in the end the Cromwellians accepted Sarah's suggestion that it had been carried away in the night by a horse thief. As compensation they made off with the animal they had seen when they first arrived, telling Sarah that in future she should take greater care of her guests' property. Laughing at their little joke, they then rode off, little suspecting how they had been duped.

Chastleton's secret room is on show to all tourists who visit the charming old house. The chamber is more comfortable than it was at the time of Arthur Jones' adventure, for the walls have been panelled and a window inserted. The entrance, too, has been altered. When it was first built there was probably a false cupboard where the present door now hangs.

Another well-known Civil War escape story concerns Major Thomas Smallman of Wilderhope Manor in Shropshire. He was captured by Roundhead troops and locked into an upper room of his own house. The Smallmans were an established recusant family, however, and Major Thomas was aware of the possible escape routes which the building afforded. While his captors stood guard outside his door, he slipped down a conveniently positioned latrine chute, seized a horse and galloped off into the distance, pursued a few minutes later by a troop of irate Parliamentarians. Soon Smallman found himself at the rim of Wenlock Edge. Before him was a sheer precipice, behind him the fast-closing Roundheads. Nothing daunted, he set his spurs to his horse and leapt into the void. Though the unfortunate animal was killed, its rider was miraculously saved when the branches of an overhanging crap-apple tree broke his fall. Since his pursuers thought it wise not to attempt a similar act of devilry, the major escaped to tell his story.

Though men such as Colonel Jones and Major Smallman had a difficult time avoiding capture by Parliamentary forces, their tribulations were nothing compared with the adventures and hardships experienced by the most famous of all Cavalier escapees, King Charles II.

The Stewarts and their Anglo-Scottish successors, the Stuarts, were not a happy breed of monarchs. Two were murdered, two were executed, one was killed in battle, and another was blown to bits by one of his own cannon. Of the nine who were fortunate enough to have passed away in their beds, two died of broken hearts, one perished as the result of a riding accident, and another breathed his last in the knowledge that his incompetence had cost him not just one throne, but two. The first Stewart bequeathed to his son a kingdom in which the normal functions of government had all but ceased, and three others failed to leave legitimate heirs.

Though Charles is included in this last trio of defaulters, it was not through any shortcoming of his own: numerous royal bastards sprang from his notoriously fertile loins. And in 1685, at the end of a surprisingly felicitous and successful reign, he left his brother with a stable, solvent and well-administered realm. The relative calm of Charles' final years, however, would have been hard to predict when the young man came into his inheritance after the beheading of his father in 1649. Indeed, following Charles II's defeat at Worcester in September 1651 he came perilously close to joining his father in the catalogue of Stewart failures. The story of how he evaded capture by the Roundheads and eventually made his way to France is a remarkable tale of loyalty, ingenuity and luck, spiced with irony by the king's frequent use of Roman Catholic hides constructed to deceive the officers of his ancestor, Queen Elizabeth I.

Civil war broke out in England in August 1642. Two

months later the 12-year-old Prince Charles was present at Edgehill to witness the first major engagement between the Royalists and the Parliamentarians. In 1645, with the war drifting to its bitter close, Charles was put in nominal command of his father's forces in the south-west, which were trying in vain to resist the advance of the professional New Model Army. The prince saw his father for the last time on 4 March. Thereafter the news was all bad. The king was soundly defeated at Naseby in June; Bristol fell to the Roundheads in August; Montrose (the outstanding Royalist commander in Scotland) was overcome at Philiphaugh a month later, and early in 1646 the Parliamentary forces in the south-west were victorious at Torrington. One by one the leading Cavaliers fled to the continent.

For a long time Charles resisted his father's instruction to join his mother in France. But now, with a Parliamentary army under the command of Sir Thomas Fairfax only 32 kilometres from the royal base at Pendennis Castle outside Falmouth, the prince was forced to look to his own safety. At the age of fifteen he experienced for the first time what it was like to be a wanted man. He crossed the Cornish peninsular to Padstow, where he probably sheltered in Prideaux Place, a fine Elizabethan mansion on the outskirts of the village.

The trouble with this part of the story is that the Prideaux family, MPs for Tavistock, were one of the few great families of the south-west who had sided with Parliament. It would be strange, therefore, if they had knowingly offered assistance to the fugitive prince. There are, however, various explanations for the rumour. Charles may have been in disguise (unlikely). Alternatively, the head of the family may have been absent on military service and, swayed by pity and inate Royalist sentiment, the remaining members of the household agreed to harbour the prince for a while. A third possibility is that the Prideaux's anti-Royalist beliefs did not extend to persecution of the king's family. The Prideaux have a fascinating collection of correspondence

conducted between their ancestors and local gentry
during the war. Its tone is surprisingly lacking in
acrimony, and suggests that the conflict in those parts was
indeed civil. The master of Prideaux Place may have been
a lukewarm Parliamentarian, prepared to hedge his bets.
The fact that the Prideaux were granted an absolute
pardon when Charles II was restored in 1660 may not have
been wholly unrelated to what had happened sixteen
years previously.

Prideaux Place is open to the public, and visitors can see
the remains of a heavily carved bed in which the young
prince is supposed to have slept. More interesting still are
persistent rumours of a secret passage (probably
incorporating part of an ancient drain) leading from
Prideaux Place to Abbey House on the quay, some 800
metres distant. The father of the present owner of
Prideaux Place, Mr Prideaux-Brune, recalled having
explored the tunnel entrance in his youth. The passage
was filled in earlier this century when sections of it began
to collapse, endangering the deer grazing in the park. At
Abbey House, however, the beginnings of a tunnel of
some sort can still be seen. It may be that, as the pursuing
Parliamentary troops closed in, Charles was led down the
secret passage to the quay, where on 2 March he boarded
a frigate bound for the Scilly Isles. Though he was
followed and surrounded by a hostile fleet, he took
advantage of a storm which scattered his pursuers to get
away to Jersey. From here he eventually made his way to
the security of France.

Charles remained on the continent for the next four
years, a frustrated observer of the tragic events unfolding
in Britain. The only practical help he was able to give his
father was to join an unsuccessful naval expedition which
sailed to the mouth of the Thames during the Second Civil
War. When the regicides executed Charles I in January
1649 they removed the head of a man who was King of
Scotland as well as King of England, and citizens of the
northern kingdom were understandably infuriated at such
action being taken without their approval. They promptly
proclaimed Charles II as their king and invited the young

exile to take up his inheritance. The king arrived in Scotland on 23 June 1650 and was crowned at Scone on 1 January 1651. That summer he slipped past the army of Oliver Cromwell and made a brave dash into England. But disappointingly few men joined the ranks of the royal army, despite the summoning of a general muster of all men aged between sixteen and sixty for 26 August. Outnumbered and out-generalled, Charles was cornered by Cromwell at Worcester on 3 September and forced to fight. By six o'clock that evening it was clear to the king and those about him that the day was lost. It had been, as Cromwell was later to report, 'as stiff a contest for four or five hours as I have ever seen', but the strange hesitance of Leslie, the Scottish commander, and the sheer weight of numbers had eventually ensured a decisive victory for the Republicans.

The situation for the 19-year-old king was now desperate. For the second time in five years he had to flee for his life. If he had fallen into the hands of Cromwell's soldiers there was little doubt but that he would have been executed: during the six-week hunt for 'the pretender, Charles Stuart, a dark man more than two yards high' a price of £1,000 was put on his head. The penalty for those who harboured him was death.

Almost thirty years later, while attending the races at Newmarket, the king dictated his version of subsequent events to Samuel Pepys. Though time had clearly dimmed the royal memory in some areas, we are left with a remarkably clear account of Charles' adventures, recorded in the same shorthand in which Pepys wrote his famous diaries. Several other near-contemporary versions of the story help to fill the gaps left by the king and correct the parts where he was clearly mistaken. Many of the places where the royal refugee sheltered are still standing and, although not all are open to the public, it is possible to make a fascinating reconstruction of the king's flight.

Accompanied by a party of nobles and Scottish cavalry, Charles left Worcester and rode hard through the gathering gloom towards Stourbridge. The progress of the fugitives was not as rapid as they had hoped. Sticking to by-ways in order to avoid recognition, they lost their way near Kidderminster. Here the king stated that he had dropped his original plan of making for London and now wished to go to Scotland instead. There, even though he might not enjoy a warm welcome, he would at least be safe from Republican regicides. In fact Charles' intentions are hard to fathom. He was unhappy at travelling with so many companions, and he probably issued false instructions lest one of the number should be captured and reveal his true designs to the enemy. Whatever his long-term objective, however, his immediate need was to find somewhere to rest.

The Earl of Derby, who was prominent among Charles' entourage, now informed the king that he knew of an ideal place, about 64 kilometres from Worcester. Earlier that year the nobleman had taken refuge in Boscobel House, Shropshire, after his defeat by Cromwell's troops, and he spoke highly of the mansion's secluded position and several concealed priest holes. Furthermore, the royal party contained two ready-made guides in Francis Yates and his master Charles Giffard, a relative of the owner of Boscobel. So without further ado the king dropped his original guide and followed Derby's advice of making for Boscobel.

Lest the arrival of so large a band of horsemen at Boscobel should attract attention, the party decided to halt at White Ladies, a large timber-framed house erected amid the ruins of a medieval nunnery on the Boscobel estate. The domestic building has now disappeared, but the ruins of the nunnery and a church are preserved by English Heritage, as are the graves of some of the actors who participated in the drama which was now unfolding. White Ladies was inhabited by five Roman Catholic Penderell brothers, all of whom risked their lives over the next few days to help the king. The pensions which the king later granted to the brothers and their descendants as a reward for their services are paid to this day.

The party reached White Ladies at dawn on 4 September. The king now decided to dismiss his travelling companions. But, as he later recollected, it was only with some difficulty that he managed to persuade them to leave: 'Though I could not get them to stand by me against the enemy, I could not get rid of them now I had a mind to.' In the end, however, the royal will prevailed, and Charles was left to fend for himself as best he could. First it was essential that he adopt some form of disguise.

The young king cut a dashing, easily recognizable figure. He was tall and dark-skinned, with long black hair, and he carried himself with the easy grace that betrayed his courtly upbringing. Nevertheless, assisted by the willing Penderells, steps were taken to render him a little more anonymous. Soot was applied to his cheeks; his gorgeous hair was roughly cropped short, and from somewhere country clothes of a suitable size were obtained: grey breeches of coarse cloth, a leather doublet, and a dirty green jerkin. On his head the king wore a greasy soft hat, which flopped down to cover some of his face. 'As soon as I was disguised', Charles remembered, 'I took with me a country fellow whose name was Richard Penderell … He was a Roman Catholic, and I chose to trust them because I knew that they had hiding holes for priests that I thought I might make use of in case of need.'

Probably looking more like a pantomime figure than a genuine yokel, the king and his new companion left White Ladies on foot, intending to walk to London. As it was still daylight, they chose to hide until sunset in a nearby coppice. Secure for a time in this leafy hiding place, Charles pressed Penderell on the best way to get to the capital. As the man tried to think of a suitable route with safe houses on the way, it became clear to Charles that his plan was wholly unrealistic. Though honest and well meaning, his accomplice knew no one of importance, and his knowledge of the countryside to the south and east was at best fragmentary. Besides, listening to Penderell speak and noting his rustic manners, the king realized that he had much to learn if he was to avoid detection the moment he stepped into the open.

It was probably at this time, sitting in ill-fitting clothes on the damp grass, hungry and virtually friendless, that Charles realized that he would be lucky to escape with his life, let alone succeed in winning back the throne. He dropped all idea of going to London and decided instead to concentrate on saving his life. He would proceed west to Wales, where he knew he still had some support and where he could take stock of his situation. If the worst came to the worst, he could lose himself in the mountains until a vessel could be found to take him back to the continent. Having made up his mind what to do, Charles spent the rest of the day learning from Penderell how to walk with the heavy gait of a labourer and to talk in the thick accents of Staffordshire. Then, as night fell, the couple set out for Madeley, 14 kilometres to the west.

On the way Charles, clearly still finding it difficult to shake off his regal bearing, was recognized by a miller and the refugees had to sprint down a lane and hide behind a hedge to avoid capture. They entered Madeley shortly after midnight and sought the assistance of a Mr Woolfe, whose Upper House in Madeley was known to have secret hiding places. The building is not open to the public, and apparently the hides have been extensively altered by structural changes. Besides, Charles and his companion were not well received by the elderly and terrified Mr Woolfe. The king told Pepys that the gentleman 'was very sorry to see me there, because there was two companies of the militia foot at that time in arms in the town ... and that he durst not put me into any of the hiding holes of his house, because they had been discovered.' So the king spent an uncomfortable night hidden behind a pile of corn and hay in a nearby barn.

All roads to Wales from the vicinity of Madeley involved crossing the Severn by ferry. Aware of this, Cromwell's officers had taken the precaution of stationing men at every jetty and landing stage along the river. When Charles heard this he was forced to revise his plans yet again, and on the night of 5–6 September he and the faithful Richard Penderell trudged all the way back to Boscobel, arriving there at about three in the morning.

To his surprise, when Richard Penderell knocked at the door of Boscobel and enquired if it was safe for the king to enter, he found that the house was already sheltering a

Royalist refugee. Major William Careless, who had fought with the king at Worcester, had made his way to Boscobel while his master was at Madeley. At first light the two gathered up some provisions and left the house. Staying clear of the thick woods nearby, which were obvious hiding places, they clambered into the branches of 'a great oak in a pretty plain place'. Here they remained all day long, occasionally peering out at 'soldiers going up and down, in the thicket of the wood, searching for persons escaped'. Fortunately the Royal Oak, as the tree came to be known, had recently been pruned and the new growth provided those sheltering in its midst with excellent cover. The original oak was hacked to death by souvenir hunters, but the present tree was grown from an acorn taken from it and makes a fair substitute.

Charles may have snatched some sleep while hidden in his arboreal bower, but by the time he came down he was utterly exhausted and determined never to spend another night in the open. Consequently, after a hearty chicken meal, a shave and a hair cut, he was put to bed in a small secret place at the head of the attic stairs. Some controversy surrounds the hides at Boscobel, for the house is furnished with two such places and we cannot be certain which was used by Charles II. The hidey hole least likely to have been employed by the king is the more obvious one below the closet leading from the main or Squire's Room. It is a low, windowless cavity set into the chimney stack and entered through a trap-door. It is not very well concealed, however, and it has been suggested that, as with so many supposedly secret openings, its original purpose had more to do with excrement than concealment. Later, when Boscobel acquired its romantic associations, an imaginative owner converted the privy into a feature with more tourist appeal. The second of Boscobel's hiding places is probably that employed by Charles. It is only 1.2 metres by 1.0 metres across and 1.2 metres high, which is sufficiently small to accord with statements that the king (who was over 1.8 metres tall) found it decidedly uncomfortable. The long attic above the hide is said to be the gallery where Charles walked the following morning to ease the cramp in his limbs, before spending the remainder of the day resting in Boscobel's formal garden.

Boscobel House is now in the hands of English Heritage, and has recently been skilfully renovated. It is the most important shrine for pilgrims following the path taken by Charles II after the Battle of Worcester, for not only can they see the secret hide where the king sheltered on the night of Saturday 6 September, but they can also view the oak growing on the exact spot where Charles hid in the branches of a similar tree.

That night the king moved on to Moseley Court (now Moseley Old Hall, Staffordshire), riding some of the way on Humphrey Penderell's 'kinde of War-horse' as his feet had been badly blistered by the long walks to and from Madeley. Armed with clubs and bills, the Penderell brothers made up a small but ferocious escort. Moseley was owned by Thomas Whitgreave, a staunch Roman Catholic who was already harbouring the popish priest Father Huddleston. The king also met with Lord Wilmot, a nobleman who was to play an important part in his subsequent adventures.

The external appearance of Moseley Old Hall has changed considerably since the seventeenth century, but some of the interior remains as it was in Charles' time. The house has at least three hides. One in the attic is not open to public view, but a small space for vestments within a roof gable and a larger opening, beneath a cupboard in the bedroom used by the king, are both plainly visible. The bed on which Charles slept is also on show. Unlike Boscobel, Moseley's hide is too well documented for there to be any doubt that visitors to the house can see for themselves the actual secret chamber in which Charles hid over 300 years ago. After all the discomforts he had experienced so far – tramping over the dark countryside, sleeping in a barn, spending a day in a tree and a night bent double in an airless hole – the priest hole at Madeley, with its brick seat and room to sit in comparative comfort, clearly met with the king's approval: 'They then showed him the place of retreat for avoiding surprisals, which having seen, entered into, and much approved of, he returned to his chamber.' It was just as well that the hide was secure, for during his stay at Moseley on 8–9 September Charles made good use of the device.

It was still dark when the king arrived at Moseley, and after his feet had been attended to and he had taken a quick meal, he expressed the desire 'to repose himself on a bed that night'. The next day, Monday, was spent resting and planning how Charles could continue his journey. Three of Father Huddleston's pupils kept a look out from the top of the house and the servants, instructed to buy in more food, were offered the half-truth that extra provisions were needed as a Cavalier soldier fleeing from the Worcester fray was sheltering in the house. After another night's rest in a comfortable bed, by Tuesday the king was feeling considerably refreshed. In the morning he watched from a window as the shattered remnants of his Scottish forces drifted north along the road outside. The domestic calm did not last long, however.

In the afternoon [Whitgreave remembered] as I was watching at the window, one of the neighbours I saw come running in, who told the maid soldiers were coming to search, who presently came running to the stairs head, and cried 'Soldiers, soldiers are coming,' which his Majesty hearing presently started out of his bed and ran to his privacy, where I secured him the best I could. And then leaving him, [I] went forth into the street to meet the soldiers who were coming to search, who as soon as they saw and knew who I was were ready to pull me to pieces, and take me away with them, saying I was come from the Worcester fight. But after much dispute with them ... they let me go. But till I saw them clearly all gone forth of the town I returned not; but as soon as they were, I returned to release [the king] ... and did acquaint him with my stay, which he thought long. And then he began to be very cheerful again.

Charles had been more fortunate than he realized at the time. While the rest of the soldiers were arguing in the house, the pursuivant Southall, 'the great priest-catcher', had tried a more subtle approach. He walked round to the back of the house and began to engage the servants in conversation. He 'asked a smith, as he was shoeing horses there, if he could tell where the king was, and he should have a thousand pounds for his pains.' The blacksmith, named Holbeard, would no doubt have welcomed the chance to experience the seventeenth-century equivalent of winning the football pools, but he was as ignorant as any of the other servants of the king's whereabouts. After a few more minutes' idle chatter, Southall rejoined his companions and Holbeard resumed his work.

It was now clear that it was too dangerous for Charles to remain at Moseley for much longer, and he decided to move on at the earliest opportunity. There is, however, one further incident relating to the king's sojurn at Moseley which is worth recording.

Charles owed his life at this time to the loyal bravery of his Catholic subjects. Furthermore, during his long hours of concealment, with the threat of death never far away, Charles had plenty of time and cause to consider the salvation of his soul as well as his body. So before the young man departed from Moseley, Father Huddleston considered the moment ripe for a little discreet proselytizing. He gave Charles a copy of the Catholic pamphlet *A Short and Plain Way to the Christian Faith*. Charles read it and was impressed. 'I have never seen anything more plain and clear upon this subject', he is supposed to have commented. This may, of course, have been just the sort of polite remark we all make when returning a book which has been loaned to us, whether we have enjoyed it or not. Or the story may be a fabrication, dreamed up by Catholic propagandists. But all his life the king retained a good deal of sympathy for the Catholic faith. It was, after all, the creed of his mother Henrietta Maria.

The king left Moseley in the middle of the night of 9–10 September, and made his way to Bentley, the home of the Anglican Colonel Lane. The king paused at Bentley only a brief while to change his disguise. When he departed he did so on foot, dressed in a suit of grey cloth and pretending to be William Jackson, the servant of Jane

Lane, the colonel's sister. Also in the party were Jane's cousin and his wife, and Lord Wilmot. Their destination was Bristol, where they hoped to find a ship willing to take the king to France.

The remainder of the king's adventure does not concern us quite as closely as the earliest part. The houses with secret hiding places in which he definitely stayed during the latter half of his escape are either not open to the public, or their hides have been destroyed. Nevertheless, some of the public buildings which he visited are still standing, and it would be a pity not to conclude a story which deals almost exclusively with history in hiding.

The party were two days on the road. At Bromsgrove one of their horses cast a shoe, and it fell to Charles, as the 'servant', to see that it was reshod. While the local blacksmith was at work, the disguised king, whose country accent was now quite credible, started chatting with the man. There are several versions of what passed between the king and the craftsman. One reports that the blacksmith said that there had been no further reports 'since the good news of the beating of the Rogues, the Scots'. When Charles then asked him whether he thought the king should be hanged for what he had done, the smith replied that Charles 'spoke like an honest man'. A second version of events has Charles asking the smith whether he had any news of the king, suggesting that he had made his way north with a view to returning to Scotland. 'No', came the reply, 'he rather lurks secretly somewhere in England, and I wish I knew where he were, for I might get a thousand pounds by taking him.' At this point the king smiled and turned away, leaving the smith to complete his task in silence.

The party spent the night of 11–12 September at the Crown Inn at Cirencester. The hostelry still exists, although it no longer offers accommodation. (Tourists looking for the pub, however, will be surprised to find that it is generally known locally by the name of its buffet bar, the 'Slug and Lettuce'.) From Cirencester the servant-king and his companions moved to Abbot's Leigh, 5 kilometres beyond Bristol, where Charles stayed for a few days while attempts were made to procure a suitable boat. When no such conveyance was found, and having been recognized by the sharp-eyed butler, on Tuesday 16 September the king travelled south to Trent House in Dorset, owned by the recusant Wyndham family. The building has a substantial hide, not unlike that at Moseley, but it is not open to the public. From Trent the king travelled with a marriage party down to the south coast near Lyme Regis, again hoping to find a sea captain willing to carry him to France.

The two days and nights which Charles spent on the south coast were extremely perilous. He was almost recognized by a stableman but managed to get away before the man's suspicions could be confirmed. One night was passed in Bridport at the George (now the Imperial Cancer Fund shop), which was full of soldiers. The second was spent at the Queen's Armes in Charmouth. Charles was not the last monarch to grace this popular inn with his presence, for Edward VII stayed there early this century. Catherine of Aragon, the first wife of Henry VIII, is also said to have enjoyed the comforts of the place. The present owner is delighted to receive tourists on the trail of Charles II, as long as they pay their bills – something which he believes the king did not do in 1651.

Having failed to secure a safe passage to France on the coast, Charles returned to Trent. He was now told that there was a ship at Southampton willing to convey him to safety. But before he could join her, the vessel was put to other use: 'by misfortune she was amongst others prest to transport ... soldiers to Jersey, by which she failed us also.' By now Charles was 'known to very many' in the district around Trent, so on 6 October he was forced to take to the road again, this time in the company of one Robin Philips. The men moved to Heale, a fine mansion 8 kilometres from Salisbury, complete with hidey hole. The king remembered clearly his arrival at the house:

> I came into the house just as it was almost dark, with Robin Philips only, not intending at first to make myself known. But just as I alighted at the door, Mrs Hyde knew me, though she had never seen me but once in her life, and that

was with the king, my father, in the army, when we
marched by Salisbury some years before in the time of the
war. But she, being a discreet woman, took no notice at
that time of me, I passing only for a friend of Robin
Philips', by whose advice I went thither.

After supper Charles confirmed Mrs Hyde in her
suspicions. Since she was anxious about harbouring so
dangerous a guest, the next morning Charles and Robin
Philips left the house openly on horseback and went to
visit Stonehenge. 'There we stayed looking upon the
stones for some time, and returned back again to Heale ...
about the hour she appointed; where I went up into the
hiding-hole, that was very convenient and safe, and
stayed there all alone (Robin Philips then going away to
Salisbury) some four or, five days.' Sadly Heale was badly
damaged by fire in 1830, and no trace remains of where
the king was hidden. Today only the gardens of the house
are open to the public.

On 12 October Charles finally received the news he had
been waiting for: Captain Nicholas Tattersell (whose grave
can be seen at St Nicholas's church, Brighton) had a
coastal trading vessel which he was prepared to put at the
king's disposal. At about this time the fugitive may have
moved into Salisbury for a few days, possibly sheltering in
Malmsbury House in the cathedral close. This is not
mentioned in Pepys' account of Charles' adventures, but
shortly before he died the late Sir Arthur Bryant insisted it
was true. Lord Coventry, who leased the house in the
middle of the seventeenth century, was closely associated
with Philips, Wilmot and other close friends of the king,
and he certainly met with them to raise money for the
royal cause. It is just possible, therefore, that Charles
called in on his way from Heale, though it would have
been unwise of him, to say the least, to pass through the
centre of so large a town as Salisbury.

What we know for certain is that the king visited
Malmsbury House in 1665, when the plague was raging in
London. His court may, in fact, have brought the disease
with them, for shortly after the king's arrival it was

ravaging the population of the city. On such occasions it was customary for the bishop to invite local dignitaries into the close, which was then sealed to prevent infection. It is said that Charles refused to be part of this privileged quarantine. He left the bishop's palace where he had been staying, moved to Malmsbury House, and rode out among the citizens.

Malmsbury House is open to the public on certain days during summer months. The small chamber known as Charles' bedroom was in all probability his dressing room. There is evidence of a hidey hole concealed behind a sliding panel, though it appears to have been much too small to accommodate a man of the king's stature. In the garden there is an ancient summer house, in the roof space of which a Cavalier of some distinction is rumoured to have hidden. Bottles and other items have been recovered over the years. Suggestions that the king climbed through a secret cupboard behind the wainscot and hid himself here for a while seem rather far-fetched. It would indeed be strange, if he had resorted to such a device, that he should fail to mention it to Pepys, particularly as his memory would have been refreshed by the visit of 1665.

Charles' last night before he embarked was spent at the George Inn at Bright-helmstead (Brighton). Here he was recognized by the landlord, who made clear the price of his silence. 'Who you are,' he muttered, 'whence you come, or whither you are going, I know not. Yet I pray God he may bless and preserve you. If I guess aright, I shall be an earl and my wife a countess.' If Charles remembered the story, he conveniently forgot the man's terms. The George is now the Old Ship Hotel on the seafront. Every May it is the starting point for a yacht race to Fécamp in Normandy, held to commemorate Charles' escape. Early on the morning of 15 October the king and a handful of followers, disguised as coal merchants from the Isle of Wight, boarded the collier *Surprise* off Shoreham and set sail for France. Narrowly avoiding an Ostend privateer, the king was finally rowed ashore at Fécamp in a 'little cock boat'. His first act on stepping ashore was to thank God, 'the Protector and Avenger of all Kings', for his safe deliverance.

In 1660, after almost nine years of weary and impoverished exile, Charles II returned to England in triumph. From that time forward he avowed that, come what may, he would 'never go on his travels again'. After all that he had been through, it was an understandable sentiment.

The wanderings of the Stuarts did not end with the flight of Charles II after the battle of Worcester. His Roman Catholic brother James, who as a child had also made a daring escape from the Parliamentarians at the end of the Civil War, succeeded to the throne in 1685. Within three years James II's staggering political ineptitude had so undermined his position that when his daughter Mary and her husband William of Orange invaded the country in November 1688, to the relief of almost everyone the king fled to France. Buildings associated with his two attempts at escape (much to the government's annoyance he was recaptured by some fishermen when first trying to get away) can be seen at Rochester and Faversham in Kent.

The most romantic Stuart escape story concerns James' grandson, Charles Edward Stuart, commonly and affectionately known as Bonnie Prince Charlie. Following his defeat at the Battle of Culloden on 16 April 1746, he was pursued around north-west Scotland for five months, until eventually rescued by French warships and carried to safety. Numerous places in the Highlands are associated with Charles' adventure (see gazetteer), but since the prince trusted natural places of concealment rather than man-made hidey holes, this extraordinary story lies outside the scope of this work.

6   Watch the Wall, My Darling

Right firm and true are the hearts of his crew,
And there's faith in the shouts that ring,
As they stave the cask, and drain the flask,
In health to the smuggler king.
                    From *The Smuggler King*, a traditional ballad

'The world', declared the Reverend Richard Harris
Barham in *The Leech of Folkestone*, 'is divided into five parts,
namely Europe, Asia, Africa, America and Romney
Marsh.' Although living in London when he wrote these
words in one of his famous *Ingoldsby Legends* (1840–7),
Barham was speaking from experience. He was born in
Canterbury in 1788, and while still a young man he took
up the post of curate at Ashford in Kent, only a few
kilometres from the edge of the desolate stretch of
low-lying grazing land which stretches out into the
Channel between the ancient towns of Rye and Hythe. A
few years later Barham became even more closely
acquainted with the area when he was appointed Rector
of Snargate, a tiny parish of some ninety-three souls set
deep in the heart of the marsh. While living at nearby
Warehorne he came to know at first hand some of the
region's whispered secrets and peculiar ways. He was
soon convinced that here lay a continent entire unto itself.

The best overall view of the marsh is to be had from near
the village of Stone in Oxney, which stands on the edge of
the scarp dividing the three marshes of Romney, Walland
and Denge from the rest of the country. To the south-east

the level farmland stretches like a green quilt towards the distant sea. Oxney was an island in the early Middle Ages, and it is recorded that in 892 Danish invaders landed at nearby Appledore with many ships. Since then the people of the fen have gradually taken advantage of the silting action of the currents rushing through the Strait of Dover to extend their territory further and further from the original shoreline. The rich pasture they have conquered is only just above sea level; some of it, indeed, would be completely submerged by the tide if the sea walls were breached. The polder is veined with innumerable canals and ditches, known locally as sewers, which bear evocative names such as Jury's Gut, Five Watering and White Kemp. For hundreds of years only those raised in the district knew their way through this watery maze. Even in summer months dense evening mists can descend rapidly to envelop the plain in a white shroud as fine and thick as the fleeces of the celebrated marsh sheep. Here, amid the dykes and foggy fields, smugglers were in paradise.

The Smugglers' Inn at Dymchurch is an obvious reminder of the illicit trade which once supported the economy of the region. More interesting are the churches of the marsh, many of which doubled as guardians of tea chests and brandy casks as well as of souls. Barham's Snargate is a splendid example. It is a fine Early English building, resting on a man-made mound and encircled by trees almost as tall as the church itself. Two features hark back to the time when it was known as a safe place for storing contraband. The first is a striking early Tudor representation of a ship painted on the north wall, opposite the main door. Local tradition holds that a church so decorated was safe for smuggled goods. Snargate was certainly secure, for until 1864 the eastern end of the northern aisle was separated from the rest of the building by a plastered partition, and could be entered only through a door in the north wall. This barn-like structure was where smugglers secreted their wares. The Reverend Barham says that he was often aware of strange comings and goings in the area late at night. In 1743, almost a century previously, tobacco was seized in Snargate's belfry and a barrel of Dutch gin found beneath the table in the vestry.

Even more unusual is the delightful little church at Fairfield, only a few kilometres to the west. It too is set upon an artificial mound, but, unlike Snargate, it is entirely surrounded by water-filled ditches. A number of footbridges enable one to approach the building on foot across the fields, though on some occasions local worshippers have had to make their way to church by boat. It requires little imagination to see why this islanded sanctuary made such a discreet depository for contraband waiting to be carried further inland and dispersed through the well-established network of fences. Smugglers also met at the church of Hope All Saints in New Romney, a Cinque Port and the largest town on the marsh. Revenue officers knew of the rendezvous, and it is said that one of their number once rounded up a whole gang of villains by hiding in the churchyard and overhearing their plans.

At the western corner of the marsh stands the old town of Rye. It was once a hillfort, then a thriving port at the mouth of the River Rother until the same action which formed the fenland to the east silted up the stream and left the town marooned some 3 kilometres from the receding coast. Despite this isolation from open waters, the settlement is just what one would wish a smugglers' haunt to be. The narrow streets climb between dark half-timbered and Georgian facades; tarry warehouses loom beside the quay; the masts and lines of vessels moored in the river's muddy waters clutter the skyline on the seaward side; and above the drum of the traffic the allusive cries of gulls and the unceasing rattle of rigging remind one that to the south-east, beyond the mud flats and the wide expanse of Camber Sands, the open Channel beckons.

Smugglers were not a particularly sophisticated breed. Not for them the intricate hidey holes of the likes of Nicholas Owen – they preferred to rely on natural caverns and tunnels or ordinary houses with capacious cellars. Besides, the bulky cargoes they dealt with could not normally be slipped behind a panel or carried into an attic. French brandy, for example, came in large wooden 18-litre casks known as 'ankers' which were not easily disposed of. In Rye, therefore, we find smugglers associated with places such as the Flushing Inn, a building which did not become a public house until the eighteenth century but whose deep medieval vault had been used as a depot for smuggled liquor long before that. The town's Olde Bell Inn was another popular haunt of the racketeers, and one of the few places where they resorted to camouflage to protect themselves. Bernard Wood in *Smugglers' Britain* (an invaluable companion for those wishing to make a detailed exploration of the hundreds of places associated with illicit commerce) notes that a while ago a revolving cupboard was discovered in the pub. It led to a concealed door through which bootleggers could escape to the street outside when threatened with a raid by the Revenue.

The best known of all Rye's inns is the Mermaid, a large fifteenth-century timbered building at the top of the town near the church. It is everything an English inn should be, serving good beer to customers sitting in secluded comfort and enjoying the atmosphere of a historic building. Here in the eighteenth century members of the dreaded Hawkhurst gang, a notorious band of smugglers, thieves and murderers, placed their weapons on the table before them and dared the law to interfere with their evening's enjoyment. Locals who patronized the Mermaid, whether employed by the Customs service or not, knew better than to interfere with these vicious men who could call on a small army of rogues to assist them in their endeavours and who, it is said, were so powerful that they landed their cargoes on the shore in broad daylight without fear of reprisal. One unfortunate citizen vanished from the face of the earth merely for staring at members of the gang, about whom more will be said later. When danger loomed, less confident rogues were known to have used the Mermaid's priest hole, or to have fled up the secret staircase to a bedroom on the first floor. From the cellars, it is said, there was access to a tunnel leading to the church.

Tourists setting out on the smugglers' trail could do

worse than spend a few hours exploring the dank reaches
of Romney Marsh, then pass the evening mulling over the
discoveries of the day in front of a warm fire in the
Mermaid. As the darkness draws in, however, and a rising
south-westerly chatters at the windows, they should not
be surprised to hear the timbers of the old building
echoing to the sound of rolling barrels – it is probably only
the barman bringing up fresh beer from the cellar. And
those quaint bearded figures at the next table, with
caloused hands and salt on their eyebrows, are just local
sailors calling in for a little refreshment after a long day at
sea. Or are they? On a dark winter's night in Rye the past
and the present become disconcertingly confused.
Though long since dead, the smugglers of the Mermaid
tavern are never far away.

Books on smuggling divide into two distinct categories.
First there are the straightforward accounts of the trade,
often written by ex-Customs officers who have no time for
lawbreakers of any description or in any age. Their
laudable standpoint is based upon their own experiences
with the professional crooks they have encountered in the
course of their duty, and is discernible in their attitude
towards smuggling in the past. Sure enough, they are
quick to find evidence suggesting that all smugglers were
callous cheats, quite prepared to murder or maim in order
to protect themselves and their contraband. They
invariably seize on the activities of the infamous
Hawkhurst gang, whom we have already encountered at
the Mermaid in Rye.

The pretty Kent village of Hawkhurst lies at the edge of
a stretch of open countryside known as the Moor, beside
the broad valley of the Rother. A more genteel community
one could hardly imagine. In the 1730s and 40s, however,
the settlement had none of its present-day graciousness,
for it was plagued by the activities of Thomas Kingsmill
and his dastardly Hawkhurst gang.

The band began as smugglers, operating on Romney
Marsh. In time, as they grew richer and more confident,
they extended their activities to include extortion, theft
and other criminal activities. They also spread the base of

their smuggling along the coast as far as Dorset in the west and Dover in the east. The Customs officers were powerless to deal with them, as this letter from an officer based in Rochester illustrates:

> We are very much infested with smugglers [he wrote in 1740] that go in such large Bodies armed with Blunderbusses and other offensive Weapons, several of which have called at my House, swearing they would kill me or any other Officer they should meet with. About a fortnight past we had an Excise Officer shot at Plackstead ... and last Wednesday the Excise Officer of Seven Oaks was taken prisoner by upwards of 20 Smugglers, who beat him and carried him to the Bull's head at Sprat's Bottom ... Last night Mr Griffin, Supervisor of Excise, ... was Beat and Cut in so violent a manner that his life is Despaired of ... Sir, I Humbly Beg your utmost Endeavours we may be supplied with some Soldiers.

No soldiers were forthcoming.

The gang's most notorious act took place in 1748. Kingsmill was told by fellow smugglers in the West Country that a large cargo of contraband had been seized by the Revenue at the close of the previous year and was now stored in the Customs House at Poole. The Hawkhurst gang was asked if it would assist in recapturing the confiscated booty, which consisted largely of tea and brandy. Kingsmill was only too pleased to help, and, gathering together some 100 of his cronies, he masterminded a daring night attack on the warehouse. All went according to plan and the next day the gang rode back to Kent, distributing presents to the cheering crowds who greeted them by the roadside.

One packet of tea fell at the feet of Daniel Chater, a poor shoemaker from Fordingbridge who knew some of the gang by sight. When news of the outrage reached the ears of the government in London they offered a large reward for any information leading to the arrest of some or all of the criminals. Chater saw his opportunity of making a quick fortune and gave the name of John Diamond to the authorities. Diamond was duly arrested and sent for trial at Chichester, where Chater was required to give evidence before the court. Knowing what the gang might do to one prepared to testify against them, the authorities appointed a Riding Officer named William Galley to escort the informant from Kent to Sussex. The couple set out for Chichester on Sunday, 14 February. They were never seen alive again. The story of what happened to them was gradually pieced together over the next few months.

The officer and the informant stayed at a village inn on the first night of their journey. Here an old woman overheard them discussing how best to present their evidence at the forthcoming trial. Within minutes the story was all over the village, and six members of the Hawkhurst gang who resided there determined to see that the couple never reached their destination. They were seized late that night, tied onto a horse and carried out of the village, all the while being beaten mercilessly with whips and cudgels. After the vicious procession had travelled a few kilometres the assailants were exhausted. As Galley was unconscious and Chater screaming horribly, the gang decided to bring their punishment to an end. Galley was buried alive in a hole which was specially dug to accommodate him, and the miserable shoemaker was cast down a well; when he continued to shout for help stones were thrown on top of him until his cries finally ceased.

These terrible punishments marked the beginning of the end of the Hawkhurst gang. The six men who had perpetrated the murders were hunted down and executed. The men of Kent might be prepared to shelter smugglers, but they drew the line at assisting cold-blooded killers. The gang fell from favour, as was shown a few months later when the citizens of Goudhurst fought a pitched battle with the bullies in the village street, and eventually drove them from the district. Kingsmill was arrested in 1749 and hanged. With his death the eighteenth-century Mafia he had created quickly dissolved.

The second group of writers on smuggling belong to the romantic school, epitomized by Kipling's poem 'A Smuggler's Song':

Boscobel House, Shropshire: the trap-door entrance to the hide at the top
of the stairs in which Charles II spent the night of 6–7 September, 1651.
After several long and uncomfortable hours in this cramped hole, the
king, who was a tall man, eased his aching limbs the next morning by
pacing up and down the attic.

The picturesque ruins of Minster Lovell Hall, Oxfordshire. In the
eighteenth century a human skeleton was found in a walled-up cellar
beneath this impressive late-medieval manor house. Was it the remains
of Lord Lovell, the loyal companion of Richard III, who disappeared in
1487?

Fairfield Church on Romney Marsh, one of the region's several delightful churches which were used by smugglers in the eighteenth century. Since Fairfield is entirely surrounded by water-filled ditches, boot-leggers regarded it as particularly secure.

Rye's celebrated Mermaid Inn where smugglers, their weapons placed defiantly on the tables before them, sat openly discussing their business. One of the best-known smugglers' haunts in the south-east of England, the building is supposed to be riddled with secret hides and passages.

The Star and Eagle, Goudhurst, said to have been linked to the nearby church by a smugglers' tunnel. It was near here that the villagers routed the infamous Hawkhurst gang in a street battle in 1748.

Said to be the oldest domestic building in Kent, the Owl House near Lamberhurst takes its name from the days when it was used by local smugglers. Dealers in illicit contraband were known as 'Owlers' after the bird cries with which they signalled to each other.

The West Wycombe Caves cut into the chalk during the eighteenth century at the command of Sir Francis Dashwood. Though the caves were rarely used by the Hell-fire Club, the labyrinth of dark passages and caverns is well worth visiting.

Sir Francis Dashwood used to invite select friends from the Hell-fire Club to party with him in this huge golden ball overlooking West Wycombe. The famous radical politician John Wilkes recalled some particularly jolly times spent in this elevated den.

Part of the concrete reinforcement added during the Second World War to the ground floor of the New Public Offices, Whitehall, to protect the Cabinet War Rooms beneath. Though substantial, it is now thought unlikely that the concrete slab would have withstood the force of a direct hit from a German high-explosive bomb.

The massive, creeper-covered bulk of the Admiralty bunker, Whitehall, built during the Second World War. The ugly blockhouse is a sinister reminder of the horrors of aerial warfare.

One of the ninete
century casemates be
Dover cliffs which
coverted into an RAF c
centre in 1939. The cha
remains much as i
when abandoned aft

The side entrance to the cliff
terrace overlooking Dover
harbour. Set into the rock
behind this gallery are the
broad mouths of the artillery
casemates built in
Napoleonic times to defend
the port. They were later
sealed and used as secret
military operations rooms.

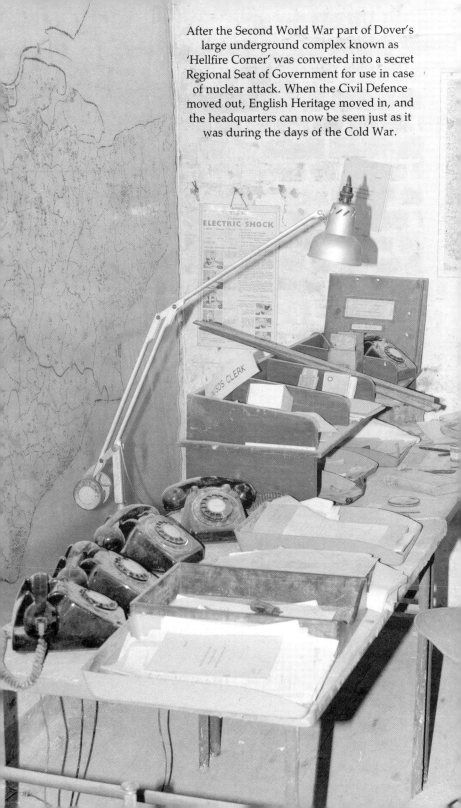

After the Second World War part of Dover's large underground complex known as 'Hellfire Corner' was converted into a secret Regional Seat of Government for use in case of nuclear attack. When the Civil Defence moved out, English Heritage moved in, and the headquarters can now be seen just as it was during the days of the Cold War.

During the Blitz several tube stations along London's Northern Line were expanded to include huge new underground shelters, some of which remained in commission into the nuclear age. The shelter at Stockwell, one of whose entrances is shown here behind the local war memorial, is now leased to a private security firm.

Inside the secret shelter added to Clapham Common Underground station at the time of the Blitz. Though extremely sordid from the outside, behind the thick steel doors the interior of the building is still kept in a reasonable state of repair. It would be useless against chemical, biological or later-generation nuclear weapons.

Them that asks no questions isn't told a lie.
Watch the wall, my darling, while the Gentlemen go by!
Five and twenty ponies
Trotting through the dark –
Brandy for the parson,
'Baccy for the Clerk;
Laces for a lady, letters for a spy,
Watch the wall, my darling, while the Gentlemen go by!

For such people the smugglers were jolly old salts who did the community a service by providing people with luxuries which they would not otherwise have been able to afford. The forces of the law are generally caricatured as bewigged busybodies and killjoys.

The truth about smugglers seems to lie somewhere between these two stereotypes. Smuggling did indeed attract criminals of the worst type – as it still does. At the same time, as all who have on occasion slipped an extra bottle of something pleasant through the Customs at Dover or Heathrow must understand, many of the thousands of smugglers were just ordinary men and women, small-scale traders or fishermen concerned only with engaging in a bit of illicit commerce in order to bring in extra cash. They were not prepared to resort to violence. To condemn as evil, therefore, all who engaged in smuggling in the eighteenth and early nineteenth centuries is to ignore or misunderstand the nature of the society in which they moved.

Britain has over 9,600 kilometres of coastline, much of it within easy reach of continental harbours. So when the government decided to impose Customs duties on imported and exported goods, in order to raise revenue and protect domestic industries, the temptations to smuggle were obvious. There was easy money to be made and no shortage of ships and seafarers prepared to run the risk of being caught. It is no exaggeration to say that smuggling was a major industry between about 1700 and 1850. It has been estimated that in the middle of the eighteenth century almost half the tea drunk in Britain had been imported illegally. Smuggling was such a commonplace activity that Parson Woodforde, an ordinary, decent country vicar, could record quite unashamedly in his diary:

> 1777 MARCH 29 ... Andrews the Smuggler brought me this night about 11 O'clock a bagg of Hyson Tea 6 Pd weight. He frightened us a little by whistling under the parlour Window just as we were going to bed. I gave him some Geneva [a spirit distilled from grain and flavoured with juniper] and paid him for the tea at 10/6 per Pd.

Since tea carried a duty of 4 shillings a pound it is clear what a bargain the parson had made. It is also clear from other entries in his diary that Woodforde was not the sort of man to have any truck with those he considered real criminals.

It is not widely known that smuggling was a two-way process. Since Tudor times, in order to assist the native spinning and weaving industries, the government made it illegal to export raw English wool. But as this high-quality commodity was at a premium on continental markets, there was always a handsome profit to be made in shipping fleeces over to France or the Low Countries from southern England. Wool from sheep raised on Romney Marsh was particularly highly prized. The most valuable trade, however, moved in the other direction.

By the eighteenth century most imported luxuries carried a high tariff, as we have already seen in the case of tea. The duty on brandy was eight shillings for 4.5 litres. This made the price of a half anker (9 litres), bought in France for sixteen shillings, at least two pounds ten shillings. The same spirit could be obtained from a smuggler at half price. Rum which cost eight shillings and sixpence from a legitimate trader could be acquired on the black market for five shillings. Similar savings could be made on the purchase of wines, sherry, port, spices, lace, silks and other finery.

For a long time the government was reluctant to spend money to stem the illegal import trade, leaving the Customs permanently short of vessels and manpower. The authorities tried to make up for this by stiffening the penalties for smuggling and associated activities. In a bout of ferocious legislation reminiscent of that aimed at recusant priests, the death penalty was introduced for both smugglers and those who harboured them, and for anyone found guilty of wounding a Customs officer or using firearms against one. As is often the case when the population feels the penalty of the law to be excessive, it was difficult to get juries to convict those accused of smuggling. This was particularly so when the men in the dock were known personally to the jury (as was normally the case in close-knit coastal communities), and when the activities of the accused were viewed not as criminal but as rendering a service. Moreover, jury members who convicted a man for smuggling had to pay more for their tea and spirits as a consequence of their high-minded action. The most unusual story of how even the highest in the land were prepared to go out of their way to protect the smuggling trade comes from a trial which took place at Ashford in 1833.

In late October the revenue cutter *Lively* gave chase to the yawl *Admiral Hood* off the Goodwin sands. The pursued vessel was returning from France, where the officers on board the *Lively* had good reason to believe that she had loaded with contraband. Their suspicions were confirmed when, as the cutter began to overhaul her quarry, a string of barrels was seen to be thrown overboard from the slower craft. The government vessel was not tempted by the bait, and in a while she caught up with the *Admiral Hood* and forced her to stop. The crew were arrested. The barrels were subsequently recovered, found to contain spirits, and the crew of the yawl charged with smuggling.

When the case came to court the Revenue officers were astounded to find Sir William Courtney, a local gentleman of some standing and an MP for Canterbury, prepared to testify on behalf of the defendants. He had been standing on the cliffs at the time of the chase, he said, and had seen all that had taken place. He was certain that the barrels had been floating in the water long before either ship came into view. The case for the prosecution seemed finished until the Treasury lawyer discovered that Sir William had been in church at Herne Bay at the time of the episode, and so could not have witnessed anything that transpired.

The smugglers were found guilty and duly punished. Sir William was jailed for perjury. He was later declared insane and committed to an asylum. Fraud though he might have been (even his knighthood was discovered to have been bogus), the case is a good example of the sort of protection afforded to smugglers by those who profited by their activities.

By the time of the Courtney case the government was finally getting to grips with the problem of illicit imports. A Coastal Blockade had been established after the Napoleonic Wars, employing ex-soldiers, known as the Warriors, to maintain a sharper watch on the shoreline. The Coast Guard had been established in 1822, funded by the Customs service but backed by the Admiralty. Thirty years later the combination of more effective policing and the government's adoption of a policy of free trade had reduced smugglers to a small number of professional criminals. That, by and large, is where the situation remains today. Of course smuggling still continues. Every now and again we hear of illegal immigrants being slipped into the country, and of the seizure by Customs of large caches of drugs and other goods. Occasionally, as in the case of the Iraqui 'Supergun' affair, officers discover attempts to export forbidden items. Dumps of explosives and weapons belonging to terrorist groups have been uncovered in woods. But modern smugglers either do not resort to caves and secret cellars, or, if they do, we are not told much about them.

Smugglers' haunts in the south-east are not just confined to Romney Marsh. The Star and Eagle at Goudhurst, the village which thwarted the Hawkhurst gang in the middle of the eighteenth century, is said to have a secret passage leading from the cellar to the churchyard a few yards away. Nearby, just off the A21 north of Lamberhurst, is the Owl House, reputedly the oldest house in Kent. The building itself is not open to the public, but the charming gardens can be viewed on 353 days of the year and have a well-deserved reputation for being among the finest in the south-east. The name of the house betrays its smuggling connections.

Those who brought contraband into the country went by several nicknames. In Wiltshire they were apparently known as Moonrakers. The term comes from a gang of smugglers who were discovered one night dragging a lake in which they had hidden some barrels of brandy. When suspicious officers asked them what they were doing, the men started to act strangely and said that they were raking the lake for the moon, whose reflection could be seen on the clear dark surface of the water. Taking them to be idiots – literally lunatics – the Customs officers smiled to themselves and went away. So the Moonrakers came into being. In other parts of the country smugglers were called Owlers. This was either because they operated only at night, or because they used the cry of the nocturnal bird as a warning call when danger threatened. The Owl House was a favoured haunt of the men who smuggled raw wool out of the country.

Filching Manor in East Sussex is believed to possess a secret tunnel dug into the side of the chalk down which rises beside the house. It was used for storing smuggled goods waiting to be distributed to other parts of the country. The Hastings Arms at Hastings, also in East Sussex, had a secret panel for storing contraband beneath the windowsill in a front room. When it was uncovered in 1961 four barrels were still there, clearly forgotten by some careless Owler many years previously. The Sussex village of Alfriston is another place famed for its links with illicit trading. Attention centres around three inns, the Star, the Smugglers' and the Market Cross. The former has an impressive carved wooden lion outside, believed to have been cut from a Dutch ship which was wrecked on the nearby coast in 1672. The villagers did not make such an open display of more valuable goods and materials salvaged from the vessel. The Market Cross Inn is supposed to have been the base of the Stanton Collins gang. Tales of secret hiding places and a concealed stairway within the ancient timber frame may have some foundation in fact, though in truth almost every pub and cellared house in the south-eastern corner of England which has stood for more than 300 years is supposed, with some justification, to have been used for smuggling.

The chalky soil beneath the Kent towns of Ramsgate, Deal, Dover and Folkestone is riddled with passages and caverns of one sort or another. Locals are never slow to ascribe the construction of these hides to their smuggling ancestors. Rumours tell of a tunnel beneath the oast house at Upton Wood. Jeremy Errand writes of a smugglers' passage leading from the cellars of the old vicarage of Holy Trinity Church at Cliftonville, and another below the cliffs of Pegwell Bay, explored by speleologists in 1970. Passing tourists are strongly urged not to undertake their own investigations without expert assistance. Further down the coast at Hastings St Clement's Caves are said to have been used by the Ruxley or 'Chopbacks' gang in the 1760s. They acquired their nickname by opening up with axes the spine of a recalcitrant Dutch skipper.

The coves and caves of the rugged shoreline of the south-west are, if anything, even more closely associated with the activities of smugglers than those of the counties nearer to the continent. It is not difficult, for example, to guess why Tea Cavern at Newquay, Pepper Cove near Padstow or Brandy Bay east of Weymouth were so named. In his *Book About Smuggling in the West Country 1700–1850* Anthony D. Hippisley Coxe devotes ten pages to listing the churches, taverns, bays and caves connected with the trade. Near Salcombe in Devon there is Tom Crocker's Hole, called after the celebrated night runner who frequented the nearby Pilchard Inn. Salcombe church was used to store duty-free goods waiting to be sent inland. On the opposite side of the peninsular there is another natural hide which bears the name of its patron. Cruel Copinger (or Coppinger, depending on which account one reads) was a shipwrecked Dane who took to smuggling to sustain himself in his exile. He based his vessel, the *Black Prince*, at Morwenstowe, where he relaxed at the Bush Inn. Several caverns in the vicinity are said to have been used by him, particularly that known simply as Cruel Copinger's Cave.

At Clovelly near Bideford (Devon) there is another cave with sinister associations. It is known locally as the Smugglers' Cave. To encourage prying locals to stay away, smugglers drinking at the Red Lion spread the rumour that the hide was inhabited by cannibals. There are plenty of caves near Bristol which were used as smugglers' dumps: some are in the Avon Gorge, others are near the old docks at Redclyffe. The area around Exeter, the second great city of the West Country and once one of the most flourishing ports in the country, is also dotted with smugglers' caves, and the city's Turk's Head Tavern was reputedly a popular rendezvous for freebooters. There are smugglers' caverns at Teignmouth and further up the River Teign at Combe Cellars. To the east, on or around the Isle of Purbeck, they used the delightful-sounding Dancing Ledge Cave, Tilly Whim Caves and Blacker's Hole.

If Romney Marsh was a separate continent in the eighteenth century, Cornwall was a different world. Novels such as Daphne Du Maurier's *Jamaica Inn* (a pub which stands at remote Bolventor on Bodmin Moor) have ensured that the county's reputation for smuggling is widely known, and today almost every bay, church and old inn boasts some link with a privateering past. Around the coast will be found the Torchlight Cave at Mullion, Yellow Rock Cavern near Fowey (where smugglers once fought a pitched battle with Revenue Officers to protect their contraband from seizure), Hell's Mouth north-east of St Ives, Seal Hole at Boscastle, approachable only from the sea, and a similar though less identifiable opening at Vugga Cove near Crantock. The caves at Falmouth were used by smugglers who conducted a thriving business in the eighteenth century under the protection of the town's mayor. The large cave at Porth Cothan was rumoured to have been linked to a nearby farm by a tunnel over 300 metres long.

The list of Cornish inns in which smugglers met and stored their wares is almost as lengthy as that of the caves they are supposed to have frequented. Among the most famous are the Jolly Sailor at Looe, where the voluminous skirts of the landlady were once used to hide a barrel of brandy from the curious eyes of the Customs men, and the Dolphin at Penzance. St Ives had three smugglers' taverns, two of which – the George and Dragon and the White Hart – are still public houses. The Halzephron Inn at Gunwalloe was once connected to Fishing Cove by a secret passage. Another tunnel in the village ran from the church to a cave on the shore. The church which boasts the most tangible links with clandestine cargoes is not in Cornwall, however, but at Kinson in Hampshire. On the parapet of the tower it is still possible to see the grooves worn by the ropes on which owlers hauled their heavy contraband to a safe hiding place in the belfry. The church at Langton Maltravers in Dorset was another hide for smuggled cargoes.

For obvious reasons Britain's western coastline is not as closely connected with smuggling as shores nearer to France and the Low Countries. However, there are some interesting stories circulating about Tredegar House in Gwent. The building has some large drains through which smuggled goods are supposed to have been brought inland from the Severn Estuary, though there is no evidence to substantiate the story. The passsages are also linked to the activities of Captain Henry Morgan, the celebrated pirate who later became Governor of Jamaica. He is related to the Morgans of Tredegar and a portrait of him hangs in the house. There is also a tradition that if one pulls the tongues of the lions' heads supporting the mantlepiece above the fireplace in the Gilt Room, the whole fireplace will swing round to reveal a secret passage. Unfortunately no one has been able to test the veracity of the story: if the lions' tongues ever existed, they were removed long ago.

Until the middle of the last century the Wirral peninsular, close to the entrance to the mighty port of Liverpool, was a renowned base for wreckers and smugglers. A report written in 1837 put its villainy on a par with that of Cornwall. Unfortunately little tangible evidence remains of this activity. The most famous smugglers' haunt was a public house known as Mother Redcaps, which acquired its name from the behaviour of its lady proprietor. When Revenue Officers were in the neighbourhood she made a point of sitting at her front door wearing a red cap as a sign of danger. Unfortunately her tavern has disappeared. What can be seen, however, are the caves in the garden of Rock Villa, New Brighton (Cheshire), which are opened to the public by their proprietor, Mr Norman Kingham. At low water sailing vessels which could not reach Liverpool on one tide had to shelter in deep pools in the Mersey. Canny locals used to misdirect vessels searching for these safe anchorages and plunder them when they ran aground. The caverns at New Brighton were used for storing the wreckers' spoils.

Evidence of smuggling is far more plentiful on the other side of the country, particularly along the Yorkshire coast. Flamborough Head, above Bridlington, is riddled with caves. As well as the rather obvious Smugglers' Cave, there are openings with evocative titles such as Pigeon Hole, Dove Cote and Robin Lyth's Hole. Almost as many stories exist about Robin Lyth as do about Robin Hood. Bullets could do him no harm, Customs men were never able to trap him and he was capable of the most prodigious feats of physical strength and skill, such as clinging to the roof of a cave in order to escape the rising tide.

The best-known smugglers' pub in the area is Three Mariners at Scarborough. It is one of the very few inns in which it is possible to find hides for contraband almost as subtle as those devised for recusants in earlier times. Though the building has only two rooms on each floor, there are two spacious hiding places. Stories of a tunnel from the cellars to Castle Hill are less easily substantiated. Locals claim that the passage remains unexplored because it is inhabited by the ghost of the headless woman. Other taverns worth visiting are the Ship Launch and White Horse (formerly the White Horse and Griffin), both at Whitby, the Ship Inn at Saltburn (whose smugglers' tunnel was explored in 1966) and the Saltergate Inn outside Whitby. The Cod and Lobster at Staithes still survives, despite being wrecked three times by the encroaching sea; but the finest of all smugglers' haunts, the Mulgrave Castle Inn, finally disappeared over the cliff during a storm in 1945. Below the Raven Hall Hotel at Ravenscar there exists a unique piece of memorabilia: a smuggler's signalling post. It is cut into the rock so that a light shining there can be seen only from the sea. When an incoming captain with a cargo of contraband saw the lantern's beam he knew that the coast was clear.

In this examination of smugglers' haunts I have allowed myself to wander slightly from my brief by referring to caves as well as to constructed hidey holes. This may be the place, therefore, to cast a quick eye over some of nature's hiding places which have featured in our history. The obvious starting point is Sherwood Forest, the home of Robin Hood, a figure who remains as elusive to today's scholars as he was to the men of the Sheriff of Nottingham in the Middle Ages. No one is sure who the outlaw really was, or even whether he existed in the flesh at all. Be that as it may, the Ollerton Sherwood Forest Centre still proudly displays the Major Oak in which Robin and his merry men are supposed to have sheltered. One wonders whether, by selecting an oak tree in which to conceal himself, Charles II had deliberately linked himself to one of his nation's most celebrated heroes?

In Wales it is not trees but mountains which have often sheltered the country's favourites. Within the lofty Carneddau range of North Wales stands a peak named Dafydd. The name recalls that of the last Welsh prince, who in 1282 hid on the mountain's bleak slopes until betrayed to the English by his own men. He was then led off to London where he met with a cruel traitor's death.

Like the Welsh, the Scots too preferred to seek refuge in their wild landscape rather than in artificial hides. To the stories of the Covenanters and Bonnie Prince Charlie (mentioned in Chapters 4 and 5) we might add that of Robert the Bruce and his well-known encounter with a spider while hiding in a cave, and the remarkable piece of escapology by William Wallace, who concealed himself and 300 of his men in a giant yew tree. A descendant of the original tree can be seen at Elderslie in Strathclyde region. The most gruesome Scottish hiding place of all is a cave beneath Benane Head, south of Ballantrae. Four hundred years ago this dank hole was the home of the Bean clan, who robbed travellers on the road above and survived by eating their flesh.

Before we draw a discreet curtain over the hides of the criminal fraternity, mention ought to be made of the places where more recent highwaymen and outlaws found refuge. Stokesay Castle in Shropshire, a unique example of a fortified manor house of the thirteenth century, is fronted by a charming wooden-framed Elizabethan gatehouse. Local legend tells that the place was once the refuge of an outlawed forger. Whether this be so or not, it would be a great shame to be in the vicinity of Ludlow and not pay a visit to the historic site.

Highwaymen are invariably associated with inns. The Black Horse in London's Broadway may have been named after Dick Turpin's mount, Black Bess. The dashing Claude Duval, a villain who in the reign of Charles II stole the purses of rich gentlemen and the hearts of all ladies who met him, was eventually cornered at the Hole-in-the-Wall in the Strand. The famous ride from London to York in fifteen hours was undertaken not by Dick Turpin (as some would have us believe), but by a Yorkshireman named John Nevison. 'Swift Nick', as Charles II dubbed him, was arrested in a secret lair in the Three Houses Inn at Sandal in his native county. The Choughs Hotel in Chard, Somerset, once possessed no less than three secret hiding places in which favoured highway robbers were afforded protection. In the seventeenth century travellers on the road between Oxford and London were kept on their toes by Jack Shrimpton and his gang of thieves. When not telling his victims to 'Stand and deliver!' Jack hid and counted his takings in the Bull Hotel at Gerrards Cross in Buckinghamshire.

Dick Turpin, a name known to every schoolboy in the land, was born at Hempstead in Essex. In the nearby village of Thaxted a building known as Turpin's House

still stands. The highwayman used it as a staging post
when he was being pursued by the law. He would enter
the stables riding a horse of one colour, then leave a few
seconds later on a mount of a different hue. He lived in a
cave in the middle of Epping Forest, but sadly this hide
cannot be traced today. What can be seen, however, is his
favourite London haunt, the White Hart in Drury Lane.
On Hampstead Heath, a few kilometres to the north, the
Spaniard's Inn proudly displays a hole made by a bullet
fired by Turpin during a drunken brawl. The Green
Dragon at Welton, North Yorkshire, goes one better. Here
favoured visitors can view the trap door in the floor
beneath which the rogue sometimes concealed himself.
Since he also engaged in a little smuggling to supplement
the income he earned on the road, no doubt the hide also
served as a useful repository for contraband.

When it really mattered, however, the stratagem failed
him. John Palmer was arrested at the Green Dragon early
in 1739 and charged with horse-stealing. At York castle the
true identity of the thief was revealed by someone who
identified his handwriting. Dick Turpin, highwayman,
smuggler and horse-thief, was executed on 7 April.

7 Private Haunts

There was discovered a large vault or room underground,
in which was the entire skeleton of a man, as having been
sitting at a table, which was before him, with a book,
paper, pen, etc., etc.; ... all much mouldred and decayed.
William Cowper in a letter to Francis Peck, 1737

Besides the priest holes, sally ports and other secret
devices built with specific purposes in mind, a number of
ancient homes are furnished with hides whose function is
not altogether clear. While the smaller openings are
obviously just safes, the larger ones seem to have served a
variety of functions, some of which were distinctly
macabre. It is hardly surprising that the contributor who
provided the following piece for the Victorian *Rambler*
magazine offered neither his name nor that of his country
seat:

In the state-room of my castle is the family shield, which
on a part being touched, revolves, and a flight of steps
becomes visible. The first, third, fifth, and all odd steps are
to be trusted, but to tread any of the others is to set in
motion some concealed machinery which causes the
staircase to collapse, disclosing a vault some seventy feet in
depth, down which the unwary is precipitated.

The most likely explanation of how the author discovered
the sinister stairway, without himself becoming one of its
victims, is that the device existed only in an imagination
enlivened by cheap gothic novels or alcohol.

Although no stately home or castle can boast of a real death-trap on the lines of the one cited above, a number of places have secret rooms whose occupants have met with mysterious ends. The delightful Cotswold hamlet of Minster Lovell, near Witney in Oxfordshire, is not at all the sort of place one would expect to be associated with foul deeds. But at the far end of the village, behind the pretty fifteenth-century parish church, there stand the shattered remains of Minster Lovell Hall. Beneath this mansion, almost two centuries ago, a dreadful discovery was made.

The Lupellus, or Lovell, family probably came into possession of Oxfordshire estates which included Minster at some time in the twelfth century. A century or so later the manor was given the name of the family who owned it, in order to distinguish it from a neighbouring one of the same name. The ancient hall became a regular Lovell family residence in the middle of the fourteenth century. The fine hall whose ruins can be seen today was erected by William, the seventh Lord Lovell, on his return from service in France in 1431.

Francis, the first Viscount Lovell (1454–87?), was a close friend and loyal supporter of King Richard III. History has not been kind to either the last Yorkist king or his followers, and Lovell is most commonly remembered as 'Lovell that dog', an epithet which he seems to have done little to deserve. For a few years Lord Francis was one of the most powerful men in the kingdom. He fought with Richard at Bosworth but, unlike the king, he managed to escape after the battle. After remaining in sanctuary at Colchester for a while, he moved north and in 1486 participated in the dangerous revolt against Henry VII, which almost succeeded in seizing the Tudor usurper at York. Once again Lovell managed to get away, this time to Flanders. Here he teamed up with a number of exiled Yorkists in an attempt to put the pretender Lambert Simnel on the English throne. At the Battle of Stoke (16 June 1487), sometimes regarded as the final engagement of the Wars of the Roses, Henry VII overcame the last serious Yorkist threat; and for the third time in as many years

Lord Lovell was forced to flee from a battlefield on which his forces had been defeated.

Exactly what happened next to Lovell is not known. Some reports say that he was drowned while trying to cross the River Trent on horseback. Others are less sure, believing him to have made a successful escape from Stoke and hidden himself in an underground vault below his residence at Minster Lovell. In 1708, when a new chimney was being built at the hall, workmen operating in the cellars broke into a chamber which was not previously known to have existed. There they found the skeleton of a man, seated at a table on which were placed a book, some paper and a quill pen. A short distance away a faded cap lay on the floor. Unfortunately, even as the labourers stared, the mysterious remains crumbled into dust in the current of fresh air which had been admitted to the room.

Who was the unfortunate man who had died alone in that sealed cellar? Was it Lord Lovell, or was it some wretched servant who had incurred his master's extreme displeasure? If the skeleton was indeed that of the Yorkist fugitive, we can only guess how he came to be entombed in that airless pit. It is possible that when he arrived home after Stoke he was so fearful of being apprehended that he ordered his men to brick him up until the danger had passed. (Some reports speak of the vault having contained barrels of provisions.) When forces loyal to Henry VII seized Minster Lovell a short while later, they may have tortured the servants to discover the whereabouts of their lord. Perhaps, having racked out the truth, they decided to leave the miserable man to die where he was. Or, unable to find the hiding place, they may have ransacked the hall and ridden off, taking with them the servants who had been responsible for concealing the luckless viscount. Thus deprived of any means of release, Lovell perished from thirst or lack of air. Treachery is the third possible explanation of Lord Lovell's fate: having little respect or affection for their lord, after they had sealed him up his retainers may either have fled into the countryside or approached King Henry's men with the story of what they had done. To the mutual benefit of all concerned, their action was then conveniently forgotten. Whoever the man in the cellar might have been, and whatever the circumstances of his imprisonment, judging by the relaxed position of the skeleton he met his end with a quiet and dignified resignation.

There are, of course, many other stories of skeletons being uncovered in strange places. The most famous concerns the remains of two children (alleged to be the Princes in the Tower) dug up at the foot of a stairway in the Tower of London. Less well known is the discovery over two centuries ago of a skeleton in a hidden vault at Brandon Hall in Suffolk, and another at Kingerby Hall in Lincolnshire. The latter is unusual in that the hiding place chosen by the victim was right next to the fireplace. The fire was out when for some reason he was locked into the hide, but a little while later the flames were rekindled and the miserable man cooked to death. The exposure of a skeleton at Ightam Mote near Sevenoaks in Kent has been given widespread publicity through Anna Seaton's popular novel *Green Darkness*. The seated remains were those of a young girl, sealed behind a side door which once led from the buttery and kitchens to the Great Hall. Though the small dark cupboard in the panelling in which the maid was found is hardly a feature of much note, the intriguing house is an outstanding example of a medieval moated manor and well worth visiting. At present it is undergoing extensive repairs which have already uncovered a number of architectural surprises.

The chained skeleton found in a pit beneath the floor of the old gatehouse at Dunster Castle (Somerset) was that of a giant of a man, at least 2 metres tall. Men of this height are no longer unusual, but in early medieval times, when it was believed the man lived, someone of this size was a veritable Goliath and a splendid asset in battle. In his book *Secret Britain* G. Bernard Wood suggests that the skeleton may have been that of a captured foreign mercenary who had been cast into the oubliette, or pit prison, and left there to die. The Scots were particularly keen on constructing such inner prisons, and anyone making a tour of castles north of the border will come across plenty of stories of miserable offenders left to starve to death in these dark, damp holes.

Our last two skeletons belonged to Lyme Park in Cheshire and Welle Manor Hall, Norfolk. Both houses teem with hidden history. The human remains at Lyme Park were apparently those of a priest who for some reason had been incarcerated in his own hidey hole. Though for architectural reasons the hide is now filled with concrete and steel, its last incumbent still makes his unhappy presence felt by appearing in ghostly form to complain about the way his mortal life was brought to its untimely close. Another unusual feature of the house is the picture of the Black Prince hanging high on the wall of the entrance hall. The painting is hinged, so that it can be swung out from the wall. In its normal position it conceals a doorway which once linked the first-floor drawing room with a first-floor chamber in the upper part of the hall. Now that this floor has been removed, it is possible to walk through an opening in the drawing room panelling, swing the Black Prince forward, and appear in the aperture half-way up the wall of the hallway. It is said that from this precarious balcony members of the household once addressed servants gathered in the hall below. The space between the painting and the panelling was a favourite family hiding place, and they even used to shut guests in there as a practical joke. Walter Scott was shown the secret cubby hole when he stayed at Lyme Park while writing *Peveril of the Peak*. He was so impressed by it that he incorporated it into his novel *Woodstock*, which inspired some of his wealthier readers to build similar hides in their own houses.

At Welle Manor Hall the entrances to no less than four secret passages have been found. In the solar (a room at the upper end of the hall) a large medieval fireplace has been uncovered. This in itself is not all that unusual – what interests most visitors is the presence of a hagstone in the hearth. In medieval times people believed that a bricked-up fireplace was a favourite haunt for a witch, so they placed a hagstone in the void before closing it off. These magic stones were a form of witch-repellant, for it was believed that if a weird sister touched one she disappeared. The stones, which have a narrow hole in them, were also used as an early form of lie-detector: a liar who put his thumb into the hole was unable to pull it out again until he had told the truth. The stone turret staircase at the Hall also has a trip step, like the one already noticed at Penhow. The house's skeleton was found bricked up at the side of one of the bedrooms. It was that of a woman, whose spectral form still flits about the house in a blue gown. The stories about her are strangely reminiscent of those concerning Canterbury's Nell the Cook: the souls of young ladies who became involved with clerics were clearly not permitted to rest in peace (see Chapter 2).

The ghost at Athelhampton in Dorset is also connected with an unfortunate incarceration, but the apparition is totally unlike those we have met so far. Athelhampton is a fine late medieval and early Tudor mansion, with a secret staircase leading from behind the panels of the Great Chamber to the library above. The enigmatic motto of the Martin family, who built the house, was 'He who looks at Martin's ape, Martin's ape shall look at him'. The family's crest was a chained ape, and apparently it was customary for them to keep a living ape in the house. The story goes that one day the ape went missing. Somehow it found its way into the secret staircase and was shut in – perhaps by a vindictive servant tired of having to tidy up the animal's mess, or in retaliation for being bitten. Anyway, the poor beast was never seen alive again. It starved to death on the dark staircase. Now the Ape of Athelhampton joins Nell the Cook, the priest from Lyme Park and the Blue Lady of Welle Manor Hall in a ghostly quartet of entombed souls.

Quite a number of old houses have secret rooms which were constructed for purposes of security rather than concealment. At Castle Menzies in Tayside there is a small, stone-lined intra-mural chamber adjacent to the Chief's bedroom. It is not really secret but is certainly secure – it can be approached only by ladder through a trap door from the room above. It may have served as a refuge or as a strongroom for important documents and money. The Prophet's Chamber at Craigievar (Grampian

Region) is a similar kind of room, though less defensible. The purpose of the concealed hide at another of Scotland's historic homes, Stevenson House in East Lothian, is less certain. In the thirteenth century the house belonged to a Cistercian nunnery. Since then it was badly damaged (particularly in 1544 as part of Henry VIII's 'rough wooing' of the infant Queen Mary for his son Prince Edward) and it was twice extensively altered. In the 1950s the owners of the house noted that in one part of the building there was a discrepancy between the external and internal measurements. Further investigation revealed a hitherto unknown opening beneath the floorboards of a hanging cupboard in one of the bedrooms. There was no way into the space except by ladder. Such a large hidey hole must have been deliberately constructed, but no one knows when this was done or for what purpose. It may have been a priest hole of some sort, a secret refuge, or simply a safe place for valuables.

We cannot leave Scotland without reference to the secret chambers in two of her grandest castles. Fyvie in Grampian Region is a magnificent harled (roughcast) building, part fortress, part residence, based around five imposing towers. On the first floor of one of these, the Meldrum Tower, is a chamber known as the Charter Room, which once served as the laird's office. Beneath it is a sealed vault containing untold riches. The presence of the room was once confirmed when the castle's owner ordered his domestic staff to hang sheets from all the castle windows; at the end of the operation two windows remained unadorned. No further attempt was made at verifying the room's existence, for there exists a curse which states that a laird who breaks into it will die shortly afterwards and his wife will lose her sight.

This curse was confirmed in the early nineteenth century when one of the Gordon lairds of Fyvie made his way into the vault. He did not survive the year, and his wife went blind. A spendthrift descendant, Sir Maurice Duff-Gordon, also tried to get his hands on Fyvie's legendary treasure in order to pay off his mounting debts. But as his workmen were hacking away at the stonework he slipped on the drawing room floor and broke a leg. At exactly the same time his wife began to complain of eye strain. Terrified, Sir Maurice ordered the labourers to stop their explorations. Preferring to part with his inheritance rather than his life, he then put Fyvie on the market.

The secret room at Glamis in Tayside is buried deep in the thickness of the crypt walls. The dark vault acquired its evil reputation when one of the Lords of Glamis and the 'Tiger' Earl of Crawford chose it as a suitable place in which to play cards with the Devil on the Sabbath. The awful combination of gambling, profanation of the Sabbath and intercourse with Satan himself so shocked Presbyterian sensibilities that the chamber was later sealed. It has never been reopened.

The presence of a so-called secret room at the Red Lodge in Bristol can be worked out by comparing the outside of the house with the configuration of the windows inside. At some time the ceiling of the Mary Carpenter Room was lowered by about 2 metres, thereby creating a large void below the floor above. Apart from prising up floorboards, there is no way into the space, which was created as part of an early 'home improvement' scheme rather than with any more clandestine purpose in mind. The secret room at Chastleton, which we met in Chapter 5, can also be ascertained by studying the lights in the window on the left of the front doorway. Three rows are visible from the outside, but only two inside, the upper one being behind the panelling of the hidey hole on the first floor. The fairly obvious discrepancy was missed by the Ironsides who searched the property in 1651.

The existence of a priest's room at Southwick Hall in Northamptonshire has recently been discounted, but there is a hiding place over an arch, accessible from the Exhibition Room on the first floor. Like the space at Red Lodge, however, this may merely be the result of internal modifications carried out in the eighteenth century. Nevertheless, there is a story that Mary Queen of Scots' burial certificate lies hidden somewhere in the Hall. It was entrusted to one George Lynne, a nervous man who was so worried about possessing such a potentially dangerous document that he is said to have walled it up behind a sealed door. No one knows where this might be, and just to make sure that treasure hunters do not go looking for it, legend prophesies that a dreaded curse will fall upon the house's owner should anyone find the paper.

We can conclude our pursuit of secret rooms with a mention of two much less sinister creations. The first is the delightful 'Secret Walled Garden' at Norton Priory in Cheshire. The garden is not really secret at all, but is simply sheltered by woodland. The area was first termed 'secret' because for years it was derelict, overgrown and almost forgotten. Now it is open to the public and makes a pleasant change from the desperate associations of so many of the hidden places we have visited. Equally charming is the Secret Room specially created by the National Trust for children beneath the stairs at Overbeck's Museum in Devon. Young visitors to the house enjoy trying to find the room, which is filled with a wonderful collection of dolls and toys.

In medieval and early modern times, particularly in the more remote corners of the land, the household of the local lord was the political, social and legal focus of the district in which he lived. His castle or manor house served as a provincial court where justice was dispensed and favours sought. The privileged life of the baronial class carried with it certain obligations, not the least of which was that of providing hospitality. As a consequence, most great houses were not so much private homes as living communities. At the centre of each was the great hall, numerous examples of which survive all over the country. By the thirteenth century it was customary for the lord and his family to have domestic accommodation adjacent to the hall. This allowed them to retire from the public gaze whenever they wished. The first manifestation of this desire for privacy was the construction of a separate room, known as a solar, at the upper end of the hall. By the fifteenth century in most large houses the solar had developed into a number of smaller, more intimate chambers and bedrooms.

Despite the obvious attractions afforded by more

comfortable and secluded accommodation, it had a major drawback. By withdrawing from the hall, except when he was dining in public, the owner of the house had lost the opportunity of keeping a close personal eye on what was going on in the busy and sometimes excitable atmosphere of the main public room. In an attempt to remedy this situation, several buildings were furnished with discreet spy-holes through which members of the household could observe what was happening in the hall without themselves being seen. There is a good example of such a feature at Affleck (Auchenleck) Castle in Scotland's Tayside Region. Above the principal staircase to the withdrawing room over the hall and other domestic accommodation there is a small private bedroom with a peep-hole. From here one has a good view of the hall and the entrance at the far end leading from the outside. Those wishing to get to the steps leading to the rest of the castle have to cross the hall, in full view of anyone stationed in the look-out post. There used to be an even more subtle spy-hole at Elphinstone Tower (Lothian Region, Scotland). It enabled someone in a tiny Lady's Room to observe the hall through a secret window in the flue of the hall fireplace. As at Affleck, it was not possible to approach the castle's private apartments without first crossing the hall in full view of the concealed port. Unfortunately the ridge on which Elphinstone stands has been undercut by coal mining, and subsidence has caused the building to become seriously dilapidated.

Gainsborough Hall in Lincolnshire, which we have already noted for its splendid array of latrine pits and secret kitchen rooms (see page 48), also has a number of interesting spy-holes. The main hall can be watched from a shuttered opening in the solar. An even more discreet lookout could be kept on the area from a tiny trap-door in the roof space. There is a third spy-hole in an inner door leading to a chamber where Freemasons once met. Having passed through the main entrance into the lobby, visitors could then be scrutinized through the shutter before being admitted to the lodge's meeting. Similar inspection windows, forerunners of the modern wide-angle security inspection lens, can be found in many old doors.

The solar of Compton Castle in Devon is provided with windows from which it is possible to observe both the hall and the chapel. The building used to have a priest hole, too, but this has now been filled in. Visitors can detect its entrance from the chapel by following a central-heating pipe going up and through what was once the door. In Peter de Savery's excellently preserved Tudor manor house at Littlecote in Berkshire there are no tunnels or priest holes, but there is an interesting feature off the Brick Parlour: from a small secret passage one can listen to conversations taking place in the library.

Also in Berkshire is the magnificent Victorian mansion of Highclere, the home of Lord and Lady Carnarvon. It is not the sort of building one would naturally associate with secret hidey holes, as it was completed in 1842 to designs by Sir Charles Barry, who was working on the Houses of Parliament at the same time. The house takes its inspiration from sixteenth- and seventeenth-century English architecture, spiced with a dash of Italianate flamboyance. No attempt was made to create the sort of pseudo authenticity suggested by the (possibly) mock priest hole at Carlton Towers (see page 74). Nevertheless, in 1987 a most remarkable discovery took place at Highclere.

In 1907 the fifth Earl of Carnarvon (1866–1923) was sent to Egypt to recover from a serious accident. He had shown some interest in archaeology in his youth, but now, with time on his hands and a wonderful opportunity to dig for lost treasures of ancient Egypt, his childhood hobby became an obsession. Working every winter with the experienced Egyptologist Howard Carter, he devoted the rest of his life to accumulating a magnificent collection of Egyptian remains.

The Earl's first find was surprising but unremarkable – a mummified cat. This was followed over the next five years by a coffin, some jewel boxes and a number of smaller objects. In 1912–13 Lord Carnarvon and Carter found a hoard of silver jewellery, followed the next season by their first tomb, that of Amosis (1552–27 BC). In 1915 the

couple moved to the Valley of the Kings, where Carter had
previously undertaken some excavation. When they
started their work here it was thought that the site had
already been so thoroughly explored that it held few
further secrets, and for several years it appeared that this
was indeed the case. The valley yielded some funerary
objects and an interesting set of alabaster jars which had
been used for storing the oils used in mummification. But
not until 1922 was anything exceptional uncovered.

In November of that year the intrepid peer and his
partner discovered the steps leading to the tomb of Tutank-
hamun (1347–37 BC). Sadly, Lord Carnarvon never saw
the tomb itself. Four months after the first step had been
uncovered he was dead from blood-poisoning, brought on
by a mosquito bite. At the moment he died the electric
lights in Cairo went out (not an infrequent occurrence) and
back home in England his favourite dog expired. People
spoke of the legendary curse of the mummy's tomb,
though why it should have affected Lord Carnarvon and
not Carter, who went on to excavate the tomb and lived to
die in his bed in England, is not explained.

Shortly after her husband's death Lady Carnarvon sold
to the Metropolitan Museum in New York what she
believed to be almost all of her husband's Egyptian collection. And with that sale the link between Highclere and
ancient Egypt appeared finally to have been severed.

In July 1987 Henry, the seventh Earl of Carnarvon,
decided to unblock the door leading from the drawing
room to the smoking room. In doing so he came across a
secret cupboard set into the thickness of the wall. The
interior was divided into small pigeon holes, some of which
were filled with wrapped packets. When these were
opened they were found to contain priceless treasures from
the fifth Earl's Egyptian collection, gathered between 1907
and 1920. It is extraordinary to think that objects which had
been hidden for more than thirty centuries should have
been lost again in the space of only a few years. Clearly, it is
not just in ancient buildings that history lies hidden.

8   Discreet Pleasures

The excavation terminates in a large lofty circular cavern
with a vaulted roof in which is a hook for suspending a
lamp or chandelier. Here according to local tradition the
Hell-Fire Club occasionally held its meetings.

The diary of Mrs Lybbe Powys, 1796

Where the main road between London and Oxford leaves
West Wycombe there is a roundabout from which the
A4010 branches north over the Chilterns towards Princes
Risborough. Immediately after the junction a small road
on the right climbs round the wooded scarp overlooking
the town. On a clear day the attention of travellers passing
through West Wycombe from Beaconsfield will already
have been drawn towards this hill, for visible on its
summit is what appears to be a classical temple, lifted
from some dusty site in the eastern Mediterranean and
deposited with eccentric humour amid the chalky uplands
of rural Buckinghamshire. The monument's extraordinary
incongruity is enhanced by a gigantic golden ball, fastened
anachronistically to the top of the ancient church standing
behind the columns. Glistening in the pale northern
sunlight, it floats above the surrounding trees like an alien
spaceship. Strange though this sight may be, however, it
is to the hillside beneath the gilded globe that we first
direct the tourist's steps. Deep inside the chalky slopes
runs a network of caves and tunnels quite as fascinating as
the follies above.

The West Wycombe Caves attract thousands of visitors

every year. They stretch for several hundred metres into the chalky hill, looping and winding at random, sometimes broadening into wide galleries, in other places becoming little more than shafts along which adults have to proceed bent almost double. It is an eerie labyrinth, skilfully lit so explorers can see where they are going without ever being quite sure where they are. The walls are damp, the slippery pebbles beneath one's feet crunch like shingle on a beach recently washed by the tide, and the air is warm and moist. Dark openings loom on either hand. As no signs point the way to the exit, it is not uncommon to meet with bewildered families wandering about in the gloom. While embarrassed parents ask the way out, their children stare wide-eyed into the darkness.

At several points along the way plaques tell the story of the caves, while recorded music and voices enhance the forbidding atmosphere. In a grotto off one of the tunnels near the entrance a display of fibreglass stalactites and stalagmites is illuminated with coloured lights. Further on there are models of miners, children from long ago exploring the caves with candles, and famous men and women who visited West Wycombe in the eighteenth century. Copies of well-known classical statues adorn the niches set into the walls of the spacious main chamber. The thrill of visiting the caves is even greater for those who know that as recently as 1973 the largest cavern was considered too dangerous to be opened to the public, because a huge boulder had suddenly crashed to the floor, crushing the waxwork scene of a secret aristocratic dinner which had been installed there. The room was finally made safe by roofing it with a steel canopy, hoisted into place by wire ropes passing through bore holes drilled from the surface and secured by 300 gigantic stainless steel bolts.

Clearly the West Wycombe Caves are no ordinary mine shafts. Why the statues, the models and music? Why do the passages twist and turn so through the chalk, instead of proceeding straight ahead like any normal excavation? The explanation is to be found in the personality of the man responsible for their construction, Sir Francis

Dashwood, and in the nature of the secret society which
he helped found, the sinister-sounding Hell-Fire Club.

Sir Francis Dashwood (1708–81) was in many ways
typical of a breed of aristocratic eighteenth-century
politician, the like of which, for better or for worse, we
shall probably never see again. Independence was Sir
Francis' hallmark: he was of independent means, as well
as of independent thought and action. Intelligent,
energetic, witty and eccentric, he held a number of
government posts during his career, interesting himself in
causes as diverse as the militia, poor relief and the revision
of the Prayer Book. However it is not for these flashes
upon the political screen that he is chiefly remembered
today, but for his notorious private life, particularly the
part he played in several exclusive clubs. He helped found
the Dilettanti Society (still extant), established to
encourage the love of art; the Divan Club, nominally
inspired by respect for the Ottoman Empire but probably
devoted more to satirical comment on Islamic society (the
Club's minute book was known as the *Koran*) and
harmless sexual promiscuity than to genuine oriental
study; the Lincoln Club, whose suggestive symbol, a
28-metre 'land lighthouse' at Dunston near Lincoln, offers
some indication of the members' libidinous preoc-
cupations; and the renowned Hell-Fire Club, a distillation
of the more licentious features of the other three, which
emerged in the early 1740s.

The aim of the Hell-Fire Club was to enable its members
and their guests to enjoy sensual pleasures in attractive
surroundings, while protected by a degree of secrecy and
anonymity; or, as John Wilkes, probably the Club's most
famous member, more flamboyantly put it: 'a set of
worthy, jolly fellows, happy disciples of Venus and
Bacchus, got occasionally together to celebrate woman in
wine and give more zest to the festive meeting, they
plucked every luxurious idea from the ancients and
enriched their own modern pleasures with the tradition of
classic luxury'. (cited in Sir Francis Dashwood, *The
Dashwoods of West Wycombe*.)

The Club was officially known as the Knights of St

Francis of Wycombe. As this title suggests, it was unashamedly irreligious in much of its conduct. Those who attended called each other 'brother' and, like medieval friars or monks, were known by their first names and the place from whence they came. Thus Sir Francis was 'Francis of Wycombe'. The chairman of the society, elected annually, was called the 'Abbot' or 'Prior', and on formal occasions he was expected to sport a red hat, similar to that worn by a cardinal. Ordinary brethren dressed in white hats, jackets and breeches. During its heyday in the 1750s and early 1760s the Club boasted a formidable membership, including several MPs, two Oxford dons, the son of the Archbishop of Canterbury, William Hogarth (the painter), the Governor of Bengal, the First Lord of the Admiralty, and sundry other peers, poets and politicians. It also seems likely that Benjamin Franklin, the celebrated American scientist and politician, may have attended meetings of the Club in the 1770s. It is even rumoured that in 1774 the evangelist John Wesley was a guest – in a strictly observatory capacity, of course. The galaxy of celebrities surpassed any of the fictional sex-party guest lists circulating at the time of the Profumo affiar. The only difference is that the revelries of the Hell-Fire Club actually took place. Eighteenth-century society was clearly more tolerant (or the well-to-do more privileged) than is the case today.

We have no detailed record of what actually happened at meetings of the Hell-Fire Club once the formalities were over. This has given rise to all sorts of ill-founded rumours of devil worship and other sinister practices. In fact the secret society appears to have contented itself with ribald versifying, drinking and sex. It has been observed that the amount of alcoholic beverages consumed was not excessive. This was almost certainly not the result of principled temperance but a deliberate attempt on the part of the menfolk to keep themselves fit for the pleasures on offer later in the evening. The Club's motto *'Fay ce que voudras'* – 'Do what you want' – was carved at strategic points about Medmenham Abbey and its grounds, where most of the meetings were held. Latin inscriptions on statues and near secluded banks urged their readers to take literally the Club's *laissez-faire* attitude towards conventional morality. Ladies who attended the meetings remained incognito behind masks until they had been given the opportunity of surveying all the men present. This was to avoid the embarrassment (or disappointment) of suddenly coming across one's husband, or a notorious purveyor of the pox. If during the initial proceedings a lady observed someone with whom she did not wish to meet, she was permitted to withdraw quietly. After that the company arranged their pairings as they wished, except that the Abbot, as chief 'monk', was permitted first pick of the 'nuns'. There are no reports of anyone being dissatisfied with an evening in the company of the Knights of St Francis.

The links between the Hell-Fire Club and the caves at West Wycombe are somewhat tenuous. Sir Francis' motives in ordering the excavation of the warren of passages was as much philanthropic as philanderous, for they were dug at a time of high unemployment to provide work for poor men of the neighbourhood, who were paid a shilling a day for their labours. The chalk taken from the mines was used as foundation stones for a new stretch of main road between High Wycombe and West Wycombe. The old road, which followed the floor of the valley, was in a dreadful state of repair: the unmetalled surface was pitted with deep ruts and in rainy weather it deteriorated into a muddy quagmire. A series of wet summers in 1748–50 caused serious unemployment and also gave the track little chance to dry out. It became so uneven that carriages on their way to Sir Francis' estate would sometimes capsize, endangering their occupants as well as the grooms and horses. The new 5-kilometre stretch of highway, therefore, killed two birds with (so to speak) one piece of chalk: guests could journey to West Wycombe in greater comfort, and Sir Francis could be seen fulfilling his duty as a conscientious nobleman. The more elevated drive also afforded a fine view of the church and its golden ball on the hill to the north.

As in the construction of the road, so in the excavation

of the hillside Sir Francis turned necessity to his advantage. He was not content to see the workmen digging out a straightforward quarry in their search for chalk. At his insistence they delved 400 metres into the rock, producing the network of tunnels and chambers which we can visit today. When the work was in operation he probably had in mind no specific purpose for the underground passages. He was just attracted by the idea of having his own private cave, as were several others who were building or 'improving' their stately homes at this time. It was a jolly feature to show off to guests. Since the mouth of the cave was visible from his mansion on the other side of the valley, Sir Francis made the aperture into a 'Gothick' folly. Above the entrance to the caves he built what appeared to be the ruined eastern wall of a medieval church. In front of this imposing edifice he laid out a broad courtyard, into the flint walls of which he set several niches for statues. The balance of the design is marred today by the presence on the left-hand side of an undistinguished wooden hut housing a ticket office and a small café.

We cannot be certain that meetings of the Hell-Fire Club took place in the caves, although Sir Francis did use them on occasion for private gatherings. Medmenham Abbey (unfortunately not open to the public) was a far more spacious and salubrious venue for the Club than the damp caverns, whatever opportunities for clandestine assignations the dark passages might have held. But in the mid-1760s the Knights were torn assunder by the issue of 'Wilkes and Liberty'. The matter began in 1763, when the well-known radical was arrested on a general warrant for his 'seditious libels' in the *North Briton* against the government and King George III. The case rumbled on for several years, and since both Wilkes and some ministers (notably the First Lord of the Admiralty, Lord Sandwich) were fellow members of the Hell-Fire Club, the future of the society was clearly put in jeopardy.

There is a story which suggests that Wilkes' wicked line in practical jokes did not make the situation any easier. Having procured a baboon and dressed it in devilish clothing, he devised a secret mechanism which released the terrified animal during one of the Club's ceremonies. To the astonishment of the onlookers, the beast sprang from his lair and perched on Lord Sandwich's shoulders. Absorbed at that moment in the atheistic ritual of the Club, the distraught peer apparently believed that the Devil himself had been summoned. Though the confessions and cries of mercy uttered by the humiliated First Lord greatly amused his fellow brethren, the jest did little to heal the breach between the minister and his radical critic.

In 1766 Medmenham Abbey was cleared of anything which might incriminate members of the Hell-Fire Club, and from this time forward rumour insists that the Club continued to meet in the West Wycombe Caves. There is no reason to doubt that the occasional party took place there, though it is most unlikely that the caverns were frequently put to this purpose. What is beyond question, however, is that Sir Francis used to invite 'brethren' to join him in the hollow globe which he had erected above the tower of the Norman church on the hill above. Here, in what Wilkes once described as 'the best globe tavern I was ever in', five or six gathered in complete secrecy to drink, sing bawdy songs and discuss matters of political moment. The view was tremendous – Sir Francis used the vantage point to signal to a friend in Camberley, some 55 kilometres away. Sadly, owing to vandalism, the ball is no longer open to the public, but one can still climb the church tower beneath it.

The labyrinth at West Wycombe is undoubtedly the most spectacular example of a secret place used for pleasure. But it is far from being the only one. Any building associated, however remotely, with Henry VIII is assuredly furnished in the popular imagination with nooks, crannies and passages which the king is supposed to have used in his adventures with ladies of the court. There are rumours of tunnels leading from Oatlands hunting lodge, Richmond Palace, Eltham Palace, Nonsuch Palace and a host of other royal residences. And, needless to say, no sooner has the presence of a tunnel been conjectured than a story of suitably illicit behaviour also appears.

Popular though these tales of royal infidelity may be, they ignore two inescapable and interrelated facts. The first is that, apart from drains (hardly the sort of thoroughfare which a king would have deigned to use, however desperate he was to sample the favours of the damsel at the other end), virtually no secret hidey holes or tunnels exist in any of the palaces frequented by Henry. Secondly, in the sixteenth century, as in almost all centuries before the nineteenth, it was regarded as perfectly normal for a male member of the royal family to keep a mistress or two. There was rarely any need for secrecy about the relationship. Indeed, the position of mistress was highly sought-after. When exercised tactfully it brought wealth and political influence not only to the favoured woman herself, but also to her relations. The rise of the Churchills during the reign of Charles II and James II owed not a little to the charms and skills of Arabella, sister of John Churchill, the future Duke of Marlborough. Fortune certainly smiled on her family when she became the mistress of the Duke of York, brother of the king.

The nearest thing to a secret passage in any of Henry VIII's palaces is the private staircase leading from the king's writing closet at Hampton Court. It leads to the ground floor and the garden, and would have enabled the king to take a breath of fresh air without having to go through the tiresome rigmarole of walking through public rooms thronged with obsequious courtiers. Charles II, whose sexual prowess is almost as celebrated as that of Henry VIII, is also credited with having used clandestine approaches for access to his lady friends. There is said to be a secret staircase at Greenwich Hospital (part of which Christopher Wren built as a royal palace), by which Charles passed unobserved between his apartments and those of Nell Gwynne. In fact the 'Merry Monarch's' advances towards Nell and others of her kind were generally far less subtle, and certainly not so discreet.

The other royal libertine about whom there are several stories involving assignations through secret tunnels is the Prince Regent, later George IV. The only underground passage which we know George used, although it is not open to public view, is that leading from the royal apartments at Brighton Pavilion to the stables nearby, and perhaps on to the barracks in Church Street. This was constructed in 1822, when the king was a gouty and overweight man of almost sixty. The days of his amorous adventures were firmly behind him. The tunnel seems to have been constructed partly as an amusing diversion and partly as a way of enabling the king to reach the stables in the dry without being subjected to the gaze of the tourists who were continually milling about the Pavilion.

In his youth, of course, George had shocked (and delighted) Brighton with his scandalous activities, not the least of which was his secret marriage in 1785 to the renowned Roman Catholic beauty, Mrs Fitzherbert. For a while the couple lived in Brighton, renting separate but proximate residences. It was at this time that the Prince conceived the idea of a 'Marine Pavilion', the first version of which was completed in July 1787. George was later forced to renounce his union with Mrs Fitzherbert and marry Princess Caroline of Brunswick, in return for which George III agreed to settle his son's debts. The second marriage was unsatisfactory, and in 1800 George was reconciled to his original spouse. According to tradition several tunnels were built from the Pavilion to houses nearby. The most likely story is of one running to Mrs Fitzherbert's house in the Old Steine, but there is nothing visible to the tourist today to give credence to the rumour.

The royal family and the aristocracy were not alone in using, or purporting to use, secret and underground places to further their pleasure. In the nineteenth century a disused chalk mine at Blackheath in south London was converted into an underground drinking parlour. A giant chandelier was hung from the roof, a ventilation shaft dug and equipped with an enormous pair of bellows, a bar set up along one wall – and the chamber was ready to receive its first customers. The success of the enterprise exceeded all expectations. Visitors flocked in from all around, attracted by the pub's original situation and its comparative remoteness from the law. Before long the place had acquired a reputation as murky as its atmosphere. Encouraged by the perpetual night pertaining 25 metres below the ground, the drinking became excessive. There were frequent brawls, some of them alarmingly violent. Criminals began to use the cavern and local prostitutes found it an excellent place in which to tout for custom. In the end the complaints of respectable citizens dwelling nearby forced the authorities to close down the pleasure cave and seal its entrance.

The cavern was reopened in 1939, when there were plans to convert it into an air-raid shelter; but these came to nothing. In 1946 the entrance was closed once more and now no one seems able to recall where it once lay. Readers are strongly advised against undertaking amateur detective work of their own in the vicinity, for it could prove extremely hazardous.

Tourists looking for a speleological adventure in the southern suburbs of the capital are directed towards the Chislehurst Caves in Kent. These popular caverns are at least safe, even though they might not be so rich in raunchy historical association. The 32 kilometres of tunnel contain a Cavaliers' Passage, grottoes said to have been employed by smugglers, and numerous rooms used during the Second World War as bomb-proof accommodation (see Chapter 9). The oldest parts of the network are believed to have been dug some 8,000 years ago by men of the Stone Age looking for good-quality flints. The shafts they dug, known as deneholes, can be found all over south-east England. They went down to a depth of anything up to 25 metres then expanded into a cluster of clover-leaf-shaped caves. The caves at Chislehurst are so extensive that visitors are offered the choice of two tours, one brief (and cheap), the other longer and more expensive which takes them deep into the heart of this fascinating labyrinth.

We now move to hidey holes and passages which were constructed purely for innocent pleasures. Our story begins with two renowned English eccentrics: William Bentinck-Scott, fifth Duke of Portland (1800–79), whose family fortune came from the coal mines on their land, and Joseph Williamson, a Liverpool merchant who accumulated immense wealth by importing tobacco. Although the underground mazes constructed by these singular gentlemen are not now open to the general public, there are plenty of eye-witness accounts of what they looked like, and the stories attached to them are too bizarre not to be mentioned.

The vastly wealthy fifth Duke of Portland, commonly known as the 'Mad Duke', spent the last twenty or so years of his life living as a recluse on his extensive estates at Welbeck Abbey, near Worksop in Nottinghamshire. The building is now a military college. Though he was deputy-lieutenant for the county and had sat in Parliament, the duke shunned society, devoting his energies to the turf and managing his estates. He was certainly a gentleman of peculiar habits. For reasons best known to himself, he always wore three pairs of socks, whatever the weather, and carried a pocket handkerchief a metre square. It is also said that he refused to allow workers engaged on the improvements he initiated at Welbeck to show any respectful signs of recognition when they came across him. This inverted snobbery was later embellished in a number of stories circulating about the duke. One of these told that estate workers were never permitted to see their master's face. The closest they came to him was when his coach, with all but one of its blinds closed, drew up where they were working. The foreman was then summoned by a footman and told to stand at a respectful distance from the vehicle, facing a lowered window. Bareheaded and scarcely daring to raise his eyes from the ground, the labourer was succinctly addressed by an indistinct figure sitting well back among the shadows of the vehicle's interior. At the conclusion of the interview, which never lasted more than a minute or two, the duke drew the blind, settled back into darkness, and rapped on the carriage roof with his stick as a signal for the driver to proceed.

Needless to say, rumour was not slow in coming forward with explanations for the duke's behaviour. The more innocent of them said that he had been jilted in his youth (it is true that he never married) and lived out his life in a sullen depression. The most popular story was less kindly. It held that the aristocrat had been hideously disfigured by syphilis, the penalty of an immoral early life, and could not stand anyone gazing upon his mutilated face. In reality the man appears to have been just an eccentric individualist with a social conscience and sufficient means to indulge his unusual tastes. He gave generously to charity and was buried in a simple cemetry without any pomp whatsoever.

The duke's finest monument above the ground was his array of glasshouses, considered to be the most splendid in the country. But it is with what he left below the surface that we are chiefly concerned here. Beneath Welbeck Park he constructed a staggering network of passages and rooms, which occupied more space than those of the Abbey itself. There were stables, libraries, kitchens and even a gigantic ballroom, reputed to be the largest in Britain. There are stories of glorious banquets and balls taking place down there, though it is not made clear why a recluse should have indulged in such gaiety. One estate worker told his son that he remembered being a member of a gang charged with polishing the ballroom floor. A long chain of men worked across the gleaming expanse with mops and buckets of stale beer, which the duke believed to produce a brighter sheen than anything possible with conventional polish. Every now and again one of the cleaners would collapse, supposedly overcome by the alcoholic fumes but more probably as a result of taking one too many illicit swigs from his pail.

The most fantastic part of the subterranean works at Welbeck was the underground private railway, explored by Jeremy Errand and described in his *Secret Passages and Hiding-Places*. Mr Errand says that when the duke wished to leave the Abbey to travel outside the county he drove a short distance from the house to the mouth of a tunnel, where he had a special station built. The coach was put on a train and conveyed about 2.5 kilometres beneath the lake and parklands to a distant lodge. With the duke still safely ensconced within it, the coach was then unloaded and driven to the mainline station at Worksop. At least one respectable social historian embellishes the story still further. He states that the tunnel went all the way to Worksop. Here the carriage was wheeled on to a flat truck and hauled to its destination, with the duke still concealed behind his velvet curtains. A branch line of the same track carried food from the basement kitchens to the dining room.

Having made his fortune in business, Joseph Williamson retired early. Like the Duke of Portland, he was sufficiently wealthy not to have to worry any longer about social niceties and conventions. He dressed like a labourer, normally wearing the same patched brown coat, heavy corduroy trousers and stout, battered shoes. Despite his rough appearance and abrupt, forthright manner, he mixed with the highest society and was once described by the Prince Regent as the only gentleman in Liverpool – a barbed comment which may tell us more about what the Prince thought of the city fathers than of Williamson himself. The merchant had little respect for the pretensions of the pompous *nouveaux riches* with whom he frequently came into contact. Legend has it that he once invited all the city dignitaries and their wives to dine with him. When they had gathered they were ushered into a ground-floor room in which they were to eat. Here they found bare trestle tables laid with jugs of water and crude dishes of bacon and beans. Offended at what they beheld, many of the guests walked out. Only when the last of the snobs had left did Williamson smile quietly to himself and lead those who remained upstairs to a rich feast set out in the dining room.

Pretension was by no means the only thing undermined by Williamson. His chief delight was in tunnelling. He began below his house in Mason Street, Edgehill, by expanding the cellars into a gigantic warren of passages, galleries and winding staircases. As time went by he became more and more obsessed with his excavations. He employed a team of miners and bought several neighbouring houses. These were then either pulled down and rebuilt as dummy dwellings, or converted into above-ground extensions to the labyrinth by having their windows and doors bricked up. Very few visitors were granted permission to explore Williamson's extraordinary creation. The fortunate few who were permitted to enter the dark maze came back with reports of a fantastic display of cellars, caverns, narrow stairways and arches over stagnant pools, all connected by a web of vaulted paths which twisted through the district of Edgehill, sometimes rising to the top of a darkened house, sometimes delving deep into the rock below. It is said that when the tunnel for the railway line from Liverpool's Lime Street to Edge Hill was being constructed, Williamson ordered his men to burrow beneath it, as a joke. One day the engineers of the railway company were astounded to hear the noise of digging coming from below where they were standing. A few minutes later a hole appeared in the tunnel floor and some of Williamson's men crawled out, with broad grins on their faces, to pass the time of day with the astonished onlookers.

On a far less grand scale than the follies of Dashwood, Portland and Williamson are the mock-Gothic conceits at Carlton Towers (Humberside) and Aston Hall, near Birmingham. The so-called secret hide at Aston is really nothing but a cupboard beneath the Jacobean Great Stairs. But in the 1820s the occupant of the house, James Watt Junior, decided to make a feature of the opening. Playing upon the fact that there were totally unfounded but interesting rumours of a tunnel leading from Aston Hall to the nearby church, he paid the cabinet maker Richard Bridgens to disguise the cupboard entrance. This was done by making it into a chair, partly composed of earlier bits and pieces. The space behind is not really a hidey hole, and it certainly does not lead to any secret passage, but it is a perfectly harmless piece of romantic amusement.

Carlton Towers, considered to be the most complete Victorian Gothic mansion, was rebuilt in the nineteenth century as the Yorkshire home of Roman Catholic Dukes of Norfolk. It replaced a house begun in 1614 by Elizabeth Stapleton, part of which was incorporated into the Gothic structure. As one might expect from a family which for centuries had stood at the heart of English Catholicism, when the Howards built their new house in the nineteenth century they included within it a tangible reminder of less happy times: a mock priest hole. Michael Hodgetts, however, argues convincingly that the hide is in fact based on a feature of the original dwelling, and is not merely a reconstruction. If this is the case, it would have been one of the last Catholic priest holes to have been completed (see Chapter 4).

The Howards are also supposed to have commissioned the tunnel which runs beneath Albury Park in Surrey. The diarist John Evelyn had something of a penchant for secret passages, and as well as building one near Wimbledon Parish Church, he was also made responsible for the construction of that at Albury. It is supposed to lead from woods near Shere to a terrace at the northern end of the house. Though the tunnel was completed before the fierce anti-Catholic hysteria of the Popish Plot (1678–80), Henry Howard, sixth Duke of Norfolk, built it in imitation of a similar classical construction near Naples, not for security.

It is wholly erroneous to believe that the value of exercise is a discovery of the later twentiety century. Before the invention of mechanized transport and the proliferation of the office job, most of the population was unwittingly or unwillingly taking exercise most of the time. And even those leading a relatively sedentary existence, particularly the cosseted ladies of a great mansion, realized that a little gentle exercise was beneficial to the constitution. In the eighteenth and nineteenth centuries no stately home was complete without its ladies' walk. Since these did not extend very far and were never arduous, they became extremely boring to the women who were expected to stroll along them day after day. Therefore, on some estates attempts were made to make the ladies' trail a little more interesting. One way to do this was to cut a tunnel on part of the walk. This provided shelter from the sun and rain as well as giving the ladies a certain *frisson* as they stepped from the sunlight into its echoing darkness. One hardly need point out that should a man accompany a lady on one of her constitutional rambles, then the existence of a screening tunnel opened up all sorts of other possibilities. There is a very good example of a rock tunnel at Cricket St Thomas, Somerset. It is to be found in the Wild Life Park and runs from the path overlooking the Paddocks to the public viewing area adjoining the Elephant Park. At the other end of the country, at Dalkeith Country Park in Midlothian, two tunnels were cut to enliven the ladies' daily strolls. Both are rather gloomy, however, and cannot have been much fun to saunter through.

Dalkeith also possesses an extensive ice house, another subterranean feature of old houses which can sometimes be mistaken for a hide or an entrance to a secret passage. These caves were exactly what their name implies – underground stores for blocks of ice, used before the invention of mechanical refrigerators. Though almost all great houses at one time possessed ice houses, they are not particularly interesting and during this century most of them (as at Cricket St Thomas and Plas Ted in Clwyd) have been filled in or blocked up. The example at Dalkeith, however, is worth looking at for it involves not just a simple cave but several passages and stairways cut into the hill beside the palace.

9   Hidden Defences

This is the room from which I'll direct the war.
Winston Churchill, on entering the
Cabinet War Room, May 1940

There are few more enduring symbols of Britain's independence than the White Cliffs of Dover. On board the continual stream of ferries nosing into the harbour below, British people from all walks of life – holidaymakers and business executives, day trippers and seasoned travellers – are irresistably drawn on deck to gaze upon the wall of pale grey chalk looming above them. This evocative image of proud insularity also serves as a potent reminder to foreign visitors that, for all the political and cultural cross-fertilization of the last thousand years, British society remains physically and psychologically separate from the continent.

Shakespeare, whose name is recalled in one of the highest bluffs, described the towering precipices above the Channel as the outer ramparts of a 'fortress built by Nature'. But men have not been content to leave it at that. Those who examine carefully the rocky heights behind Dover harbour will be able to make out, about half-way up the cliff face, a small iron-fenced balcony. Behind it a number of dark openings stare out over the Channel.

Napoleon Bonaparte once dreamed of adding Britain and her rich colonies to his empire. In the early years of the nineteenth century he assembled a large fleet of barges at Boulogne, ready to convey an army of invasion to the shores which on a clear day were plainly visible across the narrow sea. Britain's first line of defence lay with the wooden walls of the Royal Navy. The government was prudent enough, however, not to leave matters entirely in Nelson's hands. It reinforced the defences all along the south coast, particularly at Dover. Here the castle was modernized and gun batteries constructed at shore and cliff-top level. But even these measures were not considered sufficient. In order to increase the number of heavy cannon covering the harbour and its approaches, military engineers excavated six huge parallel passages (known as casemates) into the soft chalk of the cliff. These long sloping caverns, each the size of a London Underground tunnel, were then reinforced with brick linings to enable them to withstand the vibration of gunfire. They were also provided with ventilation shafts, and linked together with communication and supply tunnels. When the construction was complete, massive thirty-two pounder cannon were wheeled into place at the mouths of the casemates, their barrels pointing aggressively over the Channel. With almost 60 metres of rock above it, the battery was safe from anything but the highly unlikely eventuality of a direct hit. As it happened, the guns were never needed to repel French troops. Had they been called upon to do so, they would have made life distinctly unpleasant on board hostile warships approaching within a kilometre or so of the shore, and they would certainly have made short work of defenceless barges.

The destruction of Napoleon's fleet at Trafalgar and the subsequent annihilation of his Grand Army on the journey back from Moscow removed all immediate danger of invasion. Over the next century Dover's network of underground works was maintained in good order so that in 1914, when Britain again became involved in a European war, they were easily converted into an arsenal, offices, stores and even an underground casualty clearing station. In 1918 the tunnels were closed down for a second time. For twenty years the damp passages remained sealed in silence.

By the summer of 1938, as the aggressive foreign policy

of Nazi Germany strained to breaking point the patience of the appeasers, the easy peace of the 'long weekend' was rapidly drawing to a close. Britain found herself once more hastily preparing for war. Gas masks were issued to the population, arrangements were made for the evacuation of children from the major centres of population, and the armed forces drew up plans for defending the nation and providing an army to fight on the continent. As in Napoleonic times and during the Great War, Dover buzzed with military activity. The Straits had to be protected at all costs in order to ensure a safe passage for convoys of merchantmen, and for vessels carrying soldiers and their equipment over to France. The overall responsibility for this operation was given to Vice-Admiral Bertram Ramsay. When his staff selected as their headquarters the ready-made and bomb-proof shelter in the cliffs, the ancient casemates were about to witness their finest hour. Once the site had been chosen, work began at once to convert it into an up-to-date command centre. Even so, in September 1939 there was no way in which anyone could have foreseen that before twelve months had passed this quiet corner of east Kent would find itself at the very centre of Anglo-German hostilities. With British shipping constantly under attack from enemy aircraft, the Channel became the most dangerous stretch of seaway in the world. The shattered remnants of the British Army were salvaged from the beaches of Dunkirk just across the water, and a few months later the Battle of Britain was fought in the skies overhead. Small wonder, then, that before long the little bastion overlooking the Straits of Dover was christened 'Hellfire Corner'. It was by this time too late to move the secret headquarters elsewhere.

There are said to be some 5.5 kilometres of tunnel within the white cliffs, although only the original level of excavation – that taken over by Ramsay in 1939 – is currently open to the public. In the second year of the war it was decided to make Dover a major combined operations headquarters, which necessitated expanding considerably the warren of tunnels and caverns. By 1945 five more floors had been added to those dug in the nineteenth century. The highest was Annexe, built as a hospital. Below this came Bastion level, an intended combined services headquarters which was discontinued in 1941. Underneath Casemate were Dumpy, Esplanade and Foundation levels, which English Heritage (who now manage the site) have unfortunately had neither the time nor the resources to open to the public.

Visitors enter the Second World War Command Centre down a tunnel leading from within the castle. What they then find is an extraordinary museum. English Heritage have decided not to attempt a recreation of Hellfire Corner as it was when Admiral Ramsay sat here long into the night planning the evacuation from Dunkirk. There is enough remaining from those testing times for the imagination to do the job for them. When the military withdrew the site was simply stripped of valuable assets and abandoned, so today's visitors can see it just as it was left. Fading signs still hang on the walls, and the old air circulation system remains as it was when it was switched off for the last time. Against the wall of one of the casemates a large sheet of glass leans precariously: it is painted with a map of south-east England on which are marked all the Second World War fighter stations. How vital that fragile pane must once have been.

When the centre was at its most busy it housed about 200 personnel from all three services. They were fed from underground canteens and slept in dormitories carved out of the chalk. There were mess rooms, wash rooms and lavatories, an electricity generating plant, a BBC studio and a small telephone exchange manned by two dozen engineers responsible for keeping the 2,600 lines open at all times. The Navy operated from the easternmost casemate, which was sealed at the end facing the sea and subdivided with wooden partitions into offices and an operations room. From an office at the seaward end, with access to a balcony overlooking the Channel, Admiral Ramsay ran his crucial operations, backed by dozens of secretaries who worked the vital telephones, typewriters and teleprinters day and night throughout the war. The adjacent casemate was used by the Coastal Artillery, responsible for deploying and managing the 4,000 gunners and their weapons who stood ready to defend the beaches in case of invasion. A further casemate was an RAF command centre, and the remainder were taken up by all the other services and equipment needed to keep an underground military headquarters operating smoothly and efficiently.

The presence of the operations complex at Hellfire Corner was a well-guarded secret. Although there was plenty of protection from bombs falling from above, the openings facing towards the sea were closed only with brickwork and would have been very vulnerable to a low-level attack. No such assault was made, however, and the complex survived the war unscathed. The Royal Navy stayed on in the tunnels from 1945 to 1958, when the centre was handed over to the Civil Defence as one of the twelve Regional Centres of Government to be used in case of nuclear attack. One cannot but wonder at the choice: a direct hit on the cliff face by a nuclear device would probably have vapourized the bunker and all its contents. Nevertheless, the operations of the centre became even more clandestine than they had been during the war, and it was not taken off the secret list until 1986. To this day visitors may wonder what mysteries still lie deep behind those mighty cliffs.

Faced with the threat of aerial bombardment and invasion, from 1936 onwards the British paid unprecedented attention to the ground beneath their feet. The result was a flurry of frantic digging up and down the land. Many of the structures produced by this outburst of excavation were simply air-raid shelters. They were in no way secret, except that they had to be camouflaged in order to make them unrecognizable from the air. The whole purpose of a shelter was that men, women and children could find it quickly and easily as soon as the sirens sounded. But the underground works at Hellfire Corner are by no means the only hidden defences left from the Second World War. The government itself desired to be furnished with secure and secret accommodation. Now, thanks to the work of the

Imperial War Museum, at the Cabinet War Rooms beneath Whitehall in London we can see for ourselves exactly what part of one of these shelters looked like.

Britain was first subjected to aerial bombardment during the First World War. Between 1914 and 1918 the Germans dropped about 300 tons of bombs on Britain, killing 1,413 people and injuring a further 3,407. By the mid-1930s it was clear that in any future war the casualties and destruction of property would be far greater than anything previously experienced – one estimate reckoned that 200,000 civilians a week would be killed or wounded by bombs. In the face of these horrifying predictions, recommendations were made to disperse government offices all over the country in the event of war. Officials were understandably anxious at the chaos which might follow such a move, and they demanded that some form of nerve centre be retained in the capital, from which it would be possible to maintain overall control of the armed forces and the civilian population. At first three bunkers were suggested, at Cricklewood, Harrow ('Station Z') and Dollis Hill ('Paddock'), but even this idea was considered fraught with communications difficulties. So in 1938 plans went ahead for an underground 'Combined War Room' in the centre of London, which could house the Cabinet as well as the Chiefs of Staff.

The site chosen was in the basement of a large government building, known as the New Public Offices, occupying a huge area between Whitehall, Horse Guards Road and King Charles Street. It was thus close to Downing Street and the most important ministries. The structure was also favoured because it had been constructed at the turn of the century around a strong steel frame, which made it less likely to collapse under the impact of a direct hit from a large bomb. As the crisis over Czechoslovakia deepened in the summer of 1938, work on the project was speeded up. Colour-coded telephones and an air ventilation system were installed, the BBC equipped a broadcasting room, and the complex was strengthened with sandbags, girders, pit props and solid doors. Provision was also made to make it proof against gas attack. All this was done as discreetly as possible so as not to draw undue public (and foreign) attention to the command centre taking shape beneath the city.

The Central War Room became operational on 27 August 1939, a week before the outbreak of war, and was first used by the War Cabinet on 21 October. Two months later its name was officially changed to the Cabinet War Rooms. By this time the bunker had been expanded and a number of improvements made. The idea of a secret subterranean command post did not appeal to Neville Chamberlain, and he visited the War Rooms on only a handful of occasions. Winston Churchill, on the other hand, was much taken with the place. It appealed to his somewhat romantic vision of what the headquarters of a beleaguered garrison should look like, and he seems almost to have enjoyed the privations of an underground existence – as long as he was kept supplied with one or two other little luxuries (a fire bucket was always placed strategically near his chair in Room 69, the Cabinet Room, so that he could safely discard his cigar ends).

One of the major improvements in the War Rooms in which Prime Minister Churchill took a close personal interest was the laying of a 0.9-metre thick slab of reinforced concrete over the top of the citadel, with the intention of making it bomb-proof. Before this was done there was always a risk that a heavy bomb falling directly on the roof of the building above might penetrate as far as the basement. Churchill was horrified to find his headquarters so vulnerable. The refuge was used not only by the Prime Minister, the Cabinet and its secretariat, but also by the Chiefs of Staff and their support services. In 1940 they were joined by the Commander-in-Chief, Home Forces, the man responsible for organizing resistance to a German invasion. It is alarming to consider what damage might have been done by a single chance bomb falling on the complex. It is reported that Churchill used to clamber about on the scaffolding while the slab was being prepared, talking to the engineers and labourers, supervising their work and making his own suggestions. He once slipped off the girder on which he was standing and fell into deep, wet concrete. Anxious workmen hastily extricated the premier before he became permanently embedded.

Even as the slab was being installed, however, serious doubts were being raised in some quarters as to its effectiveness. Modern research supports these worries: it is now thought that the concrete shield should have been at least twice as thick if it was to have provided genuine protection against the heaviest bombs. Just under 1 metre of concrete would have done little to resist the impact of a direct hit from a V2 rocket, for example.

Another change made at Churchill's express command was the provision of a private room for himself deep in the basement, right at the heart of operations. The room chosen was number 65A, which had previously served as a possible meeting place for the cabinet, then as a centre for the Joint Planning Staff. Here the Prime Minister arranged a sort of bedsitting room, with a bed and desk, and huge maps on the walls showing the country's defences and other areas of strategic importance. These could be hidden behind curtains when the Prime Minister was visited by someone who might have taken too strong an interest in the wallpaper. Churchill slept in the room on only three occasions, all during the Blitz in the autumn of 1940. He normally spent the night in a shelter specially prepared for him in a disused underground station at Down Street. By the end of the year he had moved to a more spacious suite of rooms on the ground floor of the New Public Offices, known as the Number 10 Downing Street Annexe, where he was joined by his wife. He continued to use 65A as an office, and he made a number of notable broadcasts from the desk which can still be seen at one end.

Unlike Hellfire Corner, the Cabinet War Rooms have been laid out to appear as they were durng the war. Obviously there have had to be some alterations to accommodate visitors but the overall impression is surprisingly authentic. Fifteen rooms are open to inspection. They include the War Cabinet Room itself, set out as it was for a meeting of the Cabinet at 5pm on 15

October 1940. Even the clocks show the correct time.
Churchill's Cabinet and the vital Defence Committee met
here regularly in 1940 and 1941, and on several occasions
in 1944 the Cabinet returned to the bunker when the V1
and V2 rocket attacks again made life on the surface
extremely dangerous. A few metres down the corridor
from the Cabinet Room is another room which never fails
to fascinate visitors – the Transatlantic Telephone Room.
Using a scrambler to prevent his conversations from being
intercepted, from this small chamber Churchill could talk
directly with President Roosevelt in the White House,
Washington DC. The room has an unusual clock with two
sets of hands. The black ones indicate London time, the
red ones show the time in east coast America. In 1943 the
Americans sent Churchill a new and more secure
scrambling device which, they explained, would make it
virtually impossible for the enemy to make sense of any
message sent by radio telephone. When it arrived,
however, the engineers responsible for installing it found
the machine to be larger than the Telephone Room itself.
In the end the instrument was housed in the basement of
Selfridges and connected to the Cabinet War Rooms by a
special line.

One further room in the bunker deserves particular
mention. This is room 65, otherwise known as the Map
Room. It is set out as it was in August 1945, just before it
was finally closed down. The original maps are still visible
on the walls. In fact the room was concerned with a great
deal more than just geographical location: it was the
primary centre for gathering and redistributing information continually coming in from around the world.
Personnel from all three services, working in shifts, kept
the room in operation twenty-four hours a day throughout
the war. As well as incoming lines, they had direct links
with the War Rooms of the individual services and with
Downing Street. It is no coincidence that when Churchill
moved into the Cabinet War Rooms he asked to be housed
in the room immediately alongside this vital communications nexus.

In his book *War Plan UK* Duncan Campbell suggests

that the section of the Cabinet War Rooms now open to the public represents only a small part of the underground citadel. He believes, for example, that the Cabinet Office Briefing Room (COBRA), still kept ready for use in times of civil emergency, is situated in the same complex.

What of the many other secure and secret shelters prepared for government use in London during the last war? As well as the four citadels already mentioned, there were seven other major bunkers, a network of tunnels around Whitehall and four shelters built beneath existing tube stations. On several occasions the Cabinet was urged to move from the Cabinet War Rooms to the purpose-built bunker at Dollis Hill. They met there once, but found the place so uncongenial that the experiment was never repeated. The centre is now derelict, but most of the others, such as the Admiralty Citadel on the corner where Horseguards Parade meets the Mall, are still in government use. Others are in private hands. The South Kensington War Room on Cromwell Road, used as a civil defence headquarters during the war, is now a storage annexe of the Geological Museum. The British Museum uses the Goodge Street shelter (see below) for book storage. A similar shelter near Stockwell underground station (visible, ironically enough, next to the war memorial on the traffic island before the station entrance) is the records department of Security Archives Ltd. Those interested in seeing what the shelters look like inside may wish to approach the relevant authorities and ask to be admitted. Government citadels are certainly not open to public view and therefore lie beyond the scope of this book. Duncan Campbell lists in an appendix of *War Plan UK* all the underground factories and depots used by the government in the Second World War. Where possible, he states their present function. Several of the dugouts constructed to resist the onslaught of German bombs and rockets were later converted to withstand far more terrible weapons. Many tourists must have gazed at that ugly, creeper-covered Admiralty blockhouse and wondered what on earth it is for. Perhaps one day we will be officially told.

It is common knowledge that many tube stations (about eighty altogether) were used as air-raid shelters during the Second World War. What is less well known is that new underground tunnels were dug and disused ones opened up. Long caverns were excavated beneath the platforms on both the Northern and Central Lines. They were fitted out with everything needed to maintain large numbers of people during a long raid, including medical facilities, lavatories and makeshift kitchens. Access was through two specially constructed blockhouses situated close to the regular station entrances. As well as the example at Stockwell, which has already been noted, these incongruous buildings can still be seen in other places along Clapham Road, most noticeably behind the advertising hoardings opposite Clapham Common station. Four of the tube refuges were secret, reserved for use only by government or military personnel. That below Goodge Street was allocated to General Eisenhower in 1942. Only when it was damaged by fire in 1956 were the public officially permitted to know of its existence. The disused tunnels which were converted into shelters included two passing beneath the Thames and two more which ran east of Liverpool Street. Plessey converted a stretch of unfinished Central Line into an underground factory for the manufacture of vital aircraft components. Other subterranean factories existed at Corsham in Wiltshire, Dudley and Drakelow in Worcestershire, Warren Row, near Henley on Thames (Berkshire), Rochester in Kent, and at the Longbridge plant in Birmingham. Two of these (Drakelow and Warren Row) were later designated as Regional Seats of Government in the event of nuclear attack.

It is surprising how many disused Underground stations were brought into service at the time of the Blitz. Modern travellers will search in vain for Kentish Town South, British Museum, Down Street and City Road, though they were all welcome shelters from German bombing. As we have already seen, Down Street was Churchill's favoured underground resting place.

Similar tunnelling and hasty conversion took place at

other major centres of population all over the country, though no other city could match London's network of secret citadels. The government alone undertook work at some fifty-two sites. Tunnels were opened up beneath Newcastle, Birkenhead, Runcorn and Consett. At Luton, Epsom, Portsmouth, Plymouth, and several other centres, entirely new caves were excavated. More interesting was the use of ancient passages and hiding places, several of which we have already encountered in previous chapters. There was a plan to open up that fine old drinking den, the Blackheath Cavern, and convert it into an air-raid shelter. Local authorities at Ramsgate and Dover made shelters in nearby caves, and the works beneath Nottingham and Reigate also afforded excellent natural protection.

The most famous example of an air-raid shelter created out of caves was at Chislehurst in Kent. Surprisingly, these enormous caverns were not requisitioned by the government, as they had been in the First World War, but were made available to the public through the good offices of the owner. At first just a few homeless and exhausted citizens turned up. But as news of the comfort and security of the caves spread, so more and more people arrived each night and asked to be admitted. At the height of the Blitz special evening trains were carrying hundreds of people down from the capital to spend a quiet night deep in the chalky grottoes. Adults were charged one (old) penny admission; children were allowed in free.

The enormous influx of patrons presented the caves' owner with considerable problems of organization. So he set up a Cave Committee and divided the whole complex into recreational, shopping, washing and dormitory sections. The latter were subdivided into numbered pitches (like a camp site), each supervised by a Cave Captain. Before long rules had appeared, breach of which made 'shelterers' liable to loss of their pitch:

1. No admission or re-entry to the Dormitory Section after 9.30pm ...
3. Pitches must be kept clean ...
8. Unauthorised sale of goods is prohibited ...

10. Lights out and absolute silence by 10.30 pm in the Dormitory Section.

11. Pitches must not be changed, exchanged or sold.

12. Four days absence may involve loss of pitch

14. Music must cease by 9pm ...

17. Arrive early and stay put.

Though these laws may appear somewhat draconian, they were probably necessary to maintain a degree of law and order in what had become a true underground township. Besides, at times of national emergency people will readily accept the sort of discipline which would be scorned in peace time.

Electric light, washing facilities and lavatories were soon installed in the caves, and after a while bunk beds appeared, a present from the government in recognition of the valuable work being done to protect the population. By the end of the war the community boasted its own shops, a hospital (one baby was born in the caves – a girl christened Cavina), churches, a dance hall and a gymnasium. It is little wonder that the Southern Railway often had to post 'CAVES FULL' notices at its stations, and when the hostilities ceased several shelterers were reluctant to leave their new home. The owner was no doubt sorry to see them go, too. When the last of the latter-day cavemen had gathered up his belongings, tidied up his pitch and walked out of the shelter, the proprietor sat down and wrote the government a cheque for £10,000. This handsome dividend on the profit he had made out of other people's misfortunes was partly conscience money, but also a gesture of good-natured generosity on the part of a public-spirited individual.

It was not only people who had to be protected from German bombs. When war broke out there was considerable consternation on the part of curators, artists, cathedral chapters and other guardians of the nation's cultural heritage that many priceless and irreplaceable works of art would be lost unless steps were immediately taken to protect them. What followed was an evacuation almost as remarkable as that of the children which was taking place at the same time. Some treasures did not have to travel very far. The crypt of St Paul's Cathedral, for example, was considered safe enough for some of the building's valuables. Others were taken secretly out of the capital and driven up to Lancashire. Westminster Abbey entrusted wax effigies to disused Underground stations on the Piccadilly and Central Lines. Here they sat with pictures from the Tate and the Royal Academy. The British Museum preferred a stretch of tunnel near the Aldwych for the Elgin Marbles and other valuable pieces. Part of the Windsor Castle collection was stored in caverns hollowed out from the ancient sally port which emerged between the York and Augusta Towers. There are stories that the shelter was shared with the Princesses Elizabeth and Margaret, and, for a while, with twenty-six cans of heavy water smuggled out of France in 1940 and later used in the manufacture of the first atomic bombs.

The great majority of valuable works of art were removed far from the bombers' flight paths and then buried deep beneath the surface. The most secure depository was the Manod Slate Quarry at Blaenau Festiniog in North Wales, reputed to be the deepest mine of its type in the world. Five galleries were prepared, each air-conditioned and equipped with temperature and humidity controls. Steel doors with automatic alarms were fitted to the entrances. Armed guards stood outside day and night. Was all this for a few pictures from the National Gallery, which would have been impossible to display or sell in wartime Britain? Not entirely. Alongside the Titians, the Hogarths, the Michelangelos and even the complete Rubens ceiling from the Whitehall Banqueting Hall there was stored a collection which would have made a perfect target for a daring German commando raid: the Crown Jewels. The government was as determined that these symbols of British sovereignty should remain intact as it was to defend the nation's soil. It is believed that the quarry's galleries are still maintained in good order, just in case they might be needed for storing works of art in a future catastrophe.

Some of the treasures from the Victoria and Albert Museum were placed in a limestone quarry at Bradford-on-Avon in Wiltshire, while valuable specimens from the

Natural History Museum found their way into a similar excavation at Godstone, Surrey. The medieval stained glass which adorned so many windows in cathedrals and churches throughout the country presented its keepers with real problems. Sometimes windows were removed whole; but where the lead had become dangerously fragile the lights had to be dismantled piece by piece, numbered and stored in boxes. The most popular way of ensuring that the glass was completely safe from bomb blast was to bury it in sand. This process, said to have hastened the corrosion of the older panes, is given as one reason why the fine medieval glass at Canterbury, which had been subjected to interment during the war, was in such urgent need of restoration thirty years later.

Many thousands of works of art were not buried or hidden away, but merely transferred to safer homes. These were usually buildings whose owners or trustees were accustomed to being surrounded by fine works of art. Those items from the Tate collection which were not allocated to tube tunnels were entrusted to three stately homes: Muncaster Castle, Hellen's at Much Marcle and Eastington Hall (Worcestershire). The National Portrait Gallery's collection of worthies found themselves at Mentmore, the Buckinghamshire home of Lord Rosebery, and the items from the Victoria and Albert which remained above ground were stored at Montacute House in Somerset, by courtesy of the National Trust. Other foster homes for evicted treasures were found at Hall Barn and West Wycombe Park, Buckinghamshire (the Wallace Collection), Caernarvon Castle (armour from the Tower), Haigh Hall, Lancashire (the Soane Collection) and Alnwick Castle, Northumberland (the Manchester Municipal Collection). The prison at Shepton Mallet (Somerset) was taken over as a safe refuge for the Doomsday Book and other items from the Public Record Office. Tattershall Castle in Lincolnshire looked after less important specimens from the Natural History Museum. The catalogue could run and run: whatever else the winds of war might have done, they certainly scattered the nation's treasures far and wide.

Following the withdrawal of the defeated British army from Dunkirk in the summer of 1940 there was a very real possibility that the country might be invaded by the armies of the Third Reich. Many of the preparations made to throw the enemy back into the sea were not at all secret. They included gun emplacements, blockhouses, pillboxes and tank traps at strategic points all over the country. But two aspects of the defensive arrangements are of particular interest to us here. The first is concealed fortifications; the second is the network of underground hides constructed by a special branch of the Home Guard.

Henry Wills has produced a splendid study of the UK's defences in 1940, entitled simply *Pillboxes*. The book contains a list of all the pillboxes which were built, and marks them on a map to show how they fitted into proposed lines of defence. Mr Wills also devotes a whole chapter to the way these small concrete forts were camouflaged. The results of some of the measures taken can still be seen. The simplest method of disguise was to paint the outside of a pillbox to make it look like a barn, house or garage. The technique was not particularly effective, as the true nature of the building was easily recognizable from its shape. Wills tells of a signwriter in Folkestone who decorated a box with a large PUBLIC CONVENIENCES sign and placed LADIES and GENTLEMEN notices above the doors. Only when he had finished did he realize that he had probably been wasting his time. I forgot, he mused, 'the ******* can't read English'!

More subtle disguises included pillboxes built to look like cafés, summer houses, follies, and even railway wagons and vans. There is one near Holyhead on Anglesey which is a fine reproduction of a Victorian mock-medieval fortified tower. Nearby is another 'box' looking like a cross between a Martello Tower and one of the coastal castles erected by Henry VIII. One of the more ingenious pieces of camouflaging was carried out at the neglected castle of Pevensey in Sussex, where a twentieth-century gunpost was cleverly incorporated into the medieval ruins. The men who built these pillboxes obviously enjoyed the imaginative exercise, and the work was probably useful in helping to raise morale and to employ people. But it is doubtful whether these little fortresses, however well concealed, could have done much to halt a massive German invasion.

It is difficult today to take the Home Guard seriously. Whatever scant respect it might have commanded during the war has been seriously erroded by subsequent derogatory publicity, particularly by the justly successful television series, *Dad's Army*. There was one branch of British resistance, however, which no one has mocked, partly because until fairly recently little was known about it, and partly because it was much admired. It went by the innocuous sounding name of the Auxiliary Units.

The idea of a British resistance movement began in 1938 with the formation of a secret group within the General Staff (Research) department of the Foreign Office, known simply as 'Section D'. The next year GS(R) came under the overall control of the Military Intelligence Directorate and was renamed MI(R). MI(R) was responsible for a number of different tasks, such as devising buttons containing hidden miniature compasses (for use by aircrew in case they were shot down behind enemy lines), and dealing with general security problems. But in the summer of 1940 Section D suddenly became by far the most important group which it had to oversee. The name of the resistance organization was changed to Auxiliary Units, its budget was increased considerably and many more men were recruited. Behind this burst of activity it is possible to discern the figure of the Prime Minister, who took a close personal interest in the establishment of a secret unit capable of fighting long after the Germans had effected a successful invasion. The Auxiliary Units were such a well-kept secret that the Germans knew nothing of their existence. It would have been interesting to see how they coped with the occupation of a country which had a ready-trained resistance movement in place before their arrival.

The country was divided into regions and each allocated an Auxiliary Unit officer, who was responsible for gathering together his own band of resistance fighters.

Many of the best men were plundered from the regular units of the Home Guard, to the fury of local commanders. All recruits to the new organization were vetted centrally. Those approached came from all walks of life and ranged in age from teenagers to men in their seventies. Their number included professional people, such as doctors and parsons, farm labourers and fishermen, publicans, miners and blacksmiths. All that was asked of them was that they should know the countryside well, be physically tough and resourceful, and be prepared to fight to the death for their country. When advancing German forces drew near it was planned that each unit would withdraw into a secret headquarters and lie low for several days. Then, when the fighting had died down, the men would emerge to make quick surprise attacks before retiring once more into their hides. Once the country was in enemy hands they were never to return to their homes or families. They were to know as little as possible about the activities of neighbouring units.

It has been estimated that the Auxiliary Units had about a thousand 'operational bases' by the end of the war, though they possessed less than a third of this number in 1940, when the threat of invasion was at its greatest. The bases were disguised with remarkable skill to make them virtually undetectable to any one who did not know exactly what they were looking for. They were built in woods, beneath sheep troughs, cucumber frames and boulders, and even under logs. Most of them were entered through concealed trapdoors dug into the ground. Inside they were large enough to hold about half a dozen men and their equipment. They were always kept stocked with tinned food and fresh water. By 1942 most of them were fitted with bunk beds and chemical lavatories. Not all the bases were new creations. In Kent the Auxiliary Units took over old smugglers' haunts, while in other parts of the country abandoned cellars, mine shafts and ice houses made ideal ready-made hides. Sometimes members of the public inadvertently stumbled across an operation base in their neighbourhood. The best tale of such an occurrence concerns a pair of lovers from Great Leighs in Essex.

One sunny day the couple went off into the woods, looking for a quiet spot where they could be alone. After a while they selected a leafy glade, where they lay down together. Imagine their surprise when, after a few minutes, they found that the earth was literally moving beneath them. It did not take them long to discover that the reason for their instability was the presence of a trapdoor set into the earth. They reported the finding to the police, and the local Auxiliary Unit had to find a new base.

When the war ended the government ordered the Royal Engineers to destroy all known operational bases which had been set up by the Auxiliary Units. The job was done thoroughly, so that now almost all the sites are marked by nothing more than shallow depressions. One or two survived the purge, however, and can still be seen, though they are in a dilapidated condition and are on private land. In *The Last Ditch*, a survey of the preparations made for a British resistance movement, David Lampe suggests that before it is too late one of the hides should be refurbished and turned into a public museum. All who are interested in preserving our hidden heritage would surely endorse such a call.

There is one underground headquarters used by the Home Guard which is open to the public. It is at Nunwell House on the Isle of Wight, the base of General Aspinal Oglander, who commanded the forces in East Wight. Since there was a real possibility in 1940 that the Germans might have tried to seize the island and use it as a base from which to launch an invasion of the mainland, the island's defences were particularly carefully arranged. The bunker at Nunwell, for example, was unusual as a Home Guard headquarters in that it was provided with a blast-proof wall. Even more unusual was the emergency escape tunnel dug from the cellar to the grounds outside. The cellar has been made into a small Home Guard museum and, together with the rest of the house, is open on certain days during the summer. Equally interesting, and certainly more elaborate, are the underground defences dug by the Germans on several of the Channel

Islands. Many of them are now open to inspection and make an absorbing addition to a holiday spent at those delightful resorts.

An examination of Britain's secret hiding places open to public view really ought to conclude with the arrival of peace in 1945. It is worth mentioning, however, that the story continues to unfold. Today's news is tomorrow's history. As we have seen, smugglers still ply their illegal trade, and no doubt when the history of the present wave of drug trafficking comes to be written plenty of fresh examples of hides will come to light. The same applies to the never-ending battle with terrorism. Tactics and skills similar to those employed by Nicholas Owen to conceal priests and by the Auxiliary Units to camouflage their bases are probably even now being used by criminals to hide caches of arms and explosives.

Nevertheless, there is one group of modern secret refuges which cannot be ignored completely: the underground bunkers from which the government of Britain would be conducted in the event of nuclear or biological war. Needless to say, many of these shelters are still classified as secret, although, as we saw at Hellfire Corner, in recent years the government has been more open about its civil defence preparations. We can only hope that with the steady improvement of East–West relations the need for these sinister bunkers will diminish to the point where they are no longer considered necessary.

Immediately after the Second World War little interest was shown in preserving the huge network of refuges and bunkers which had been constructed over the previous ten years. By 1950, however, with the Cold War intensifying, the government began to change its mind. Between 1950 and 1955 about 100 secret bunkers of one sort or another were constructed. Some were radar and anti-aircraft posts. Others, such as the two-storey constructions at Cambridge, Newcastle and Tunbridge Wells, were built to house Regional Commissioners and their staff, the civil servants who were to govern their areas in the event of war. The network was out of date almost as soon as it had been completed.

By 1955 the advent of the Hydrogen bomb and the

inter-continental ballistic missile had added a new dimension of horror to the prospect of future war. The area of destruction covered by the blast of an H-bomb was a hundred times that of the A-bomb. The government decided, rightly or wrongly, that there was little point in trying to provide shelter for the mass of the population in the face of a nuclear attack, and it concentrated instead on keeping some form of government running. To this end it converted the Spring Quarries outside Corsham (near Bath) in Wiltshire, which had housed an underground aircraft factory in the Second World War, into a Central Government War Headquarters of 40 hectares. Since the citadel is reported to be only about 35 metres below the surface and its presence is certainly known to the Russians, the chances of it surviving a nuclear attack are remote. Even so, the massive military complex, which can be seen (but not photographed) from the roads running through it, makes chilling viewing. Behind the barbed wire and road blocks the hillside is dotted with evil-looking concrete bunkers, some of which are clearly still under construction.

As well as an underground headquarters, the government also established Home Defence Regions, each with its Regional Seat of Government (RSG), like the one below Hellfire Corner at Dover. These were reorganized in 1973. Though the system was supposed to be top secret, several reports about it appeared in the newspapers, and the government suffered considerable embarrassment in 1963 when supporters of CND managed to break into RSG 6 (Warren Row). Some of the walkers on the 1963 Aldermaston March took a short detour from the official route along the A4 and staged a protest outside the very gates of RSG 6. So much for official secrecy.

The attention paid to civil defence appears to fluctuate according to the state of East–West relations and the viewpoint of the party in power. During the Reagan–Thatcher *entente* in the early 1980s the organization was again overhauled, though it has become increasingly clear that not one of the comparatively shallow British shelters could survive a well-directed attack. The Americans now base their survival strategy on airborne command centres. Today the possibility of a nuclear confrontation appears as distant as at any time since the start of the Cold War. The anonymous citadels are still there, of course, secure behind steel fences. And there are almost certainly some about which the public still remains ignorant. But let us hope that one day, along with the priest holes and sally ports of previous generations, even these grim bunkers will be declassified and so become merely another chapter in the long story of history in hiding.

Gazetteer

Places mentioned in the text which can be visited by the public – including open air sites to which there is access, but excluding buildings which can be viewed only from the outside.

ENGLAND

AVON

Avon Gorge
Bath Abbey
Redclyffe
Red Lodge

BERKSHIRE

Highclere
Littlecote
Mapledurham
Windsor Castle

BIRMINGHAM

Aston Hall

BUCKINGHAMSHIRE

Gerrards Cross – Bull Hotel
West Wycombe – caves and church

CAMBRIDGESHIRE

Sawston Hall

CHESHIRE

Gawsworth Hall
Little Moreton Hall
Lyme Park
New Brighton – Rock Villa Caves
Norton Priory

CORNWALL

Bolventor – Jamaica Inn
Boscastle – Seal Hole
Crantock – Vugga Cove
Falmouth – Porth Cothan Cave
Fowey – Yellow Rock Cavern
Godolphin House
Gunwalloe – Halzephron Inn
Looe – Jolly Sailor Inn
Morwenstowe – Bush Inn
   – Cruel Copinger's Cave
Mullion – Torchlight Cave
Newquay – Tea Cavern
Padstow – Pepper Cove
Pendennis Castle
Penzance – Dolphin Inn
Prideaux Place
St Ives – George and Dragon Inn
   – Hell's Mouth Cave
   – White Hart

CUMBRIA

Dalemain
Levens Hall
Muncaster Castle
Naworth Castle
Welton – Green Dragon

DEVON

Bickleigh Castle
Buckland Abbey
Bull House
Cadhay
Clovelly – Red Lion
  – Smugglers' Cave
Compton Castle
Exeter – Castle mound
  – Turk's Head
Hartland Abbey
Overbeck's Museum
Salcombe Church
Salcombe – Tom Crocker's Hole
  – Pilchard Inn
Teignmouth – Combe Cellars
Tiverton Castle
Torre Abbey

DORSET

Athelhampton
Charmouth – the Queen's Armes
Isle of Purbeck – Blacker's Hole
  – Dancing Ledge Cave
  – Tilly Whim Caves
Langton Maltravers Church
Sherbourne – Abbey
  – Old Castle
Weymouth – Brandy Bay

ESSEX

Braddocks
Castle Hedingham
Layer Marney Tower
Thaxted – Turpin's House

GLOUCESTERSHIRE

Cirencester – the Crown Inn
Newark Park
Whittington Court

HAMPSHIRE

Beaulieu Abbey
Braemore House
Kinson Church
Winchester Cathedral

HEREFORD AND WORCESTER

Harvington Hall
Hellen's, Much Marcle
Hereford Castle
Huddington Court
Worcester Cathedral

HERTFORDSHIRE

The Manor House, Chenies
St Albans Cathedral

HUMBERSIDE

Burton Constable Hall
Carlton Towers
Thornton Abbey

ISLE OF WIGHT

Nunwell House

KENT

Bayham Abbey
Canterbury Cathedral
Chislehurst Caves
Dover Castle
Dover – Second World War Command Centre
Dymchurch – Smugglers' Inn
Fairfield Church
Goudhurst – Star and Eagle

Hall Place
Ightam Mote
Leeds Castle
Owl House
Rochester Castle
Rochester – Coopers' Arms
Scotney Old Castle
Sissinghurst Castle
Snargate Church

LANCASHIRE

Chingle Hall
Hoghton Tower
Leighton Hall
Rufford Old Hall
Samlesbury Hall
Towneley Hall
Turton Tower

LEICESTERSHIRE

Rockingham Castle

LINCOLNSHIRE

Gainsborough Old Hall
Kingerby Hall
Lincoln Cathedral
Tattershall Castle

LIVERPOOL

Meols Hall
Speke Hall

LONDON

Black Horse Inn, Broadway
Cabinet War Rooms

Greenwich Hospital
Hampton Court
Hole-in-the-Wall Inn, Strand
Spaniard's Inn, Hampstead
St Paul's Cathedral
Tower of London
White Hart, Drury Lane

NORFOLK

Oxburgh Hall
Rainthorpe Hall
Welle Manor Hall

NORTHAMPTONSHIRE

Kirby Hall
Rockingham Castle
Rushton Hall
Southwick Hall

NORTHUMBERLAND

Alnwick Castle
Berwick-upon-Tweed
Capheaton
Warkworth Castle

NOTTINGHAMSHIRE

Jerusalem Inn
Nottingham Castle
Sherwood Forest Visitors' Centre, Ollerton
Southwell Minster
Thrumpton Hall

OXFORDSHIRE

Chastleton
Minster Lovell Hall

Stonor

SHROPSHIRE

Boscobel House
Ludford House
Stokesay Castle
White Ladies Priory
Wilderhope Manor

SOMERSET

Chard – Choughs Hotel
Cricket St Thomas
Dunster Castle
Forde Abbey
Montacute House
Poundisford Park
Tudor Hall

STAFFORDSHIRE

Moseley Old Hall
Tamworth Castle

SUFFOLK

Brandon Hall
Bury St Edmunds Abbey
Cavendish Manor
Kentwell Hall
Lavenham Priory
Melford Hall
Wingfield College

SURREY

Albury Park
Reigate Castle mound and Barons' Cave

EAST SUSSEX

Alfriston – Market Cross Inn
   – Smugglers' Inn
   – Star Inn
Bodiam Castle
Brighton – Old Ship Hotel
   – Royal Pavilion
   – St Nicholas's Church
Filching Manor
Hastings – Hastings Arms
   – St Clement's Caves
Hawkhurst
Parham
Pevensey Castle
Rye – Flushing Inn
   – Mermaid Inn
   – Olde Bell Inn

WEST SUSSEX

Arundel Castle
Newick Park

WARWICKSHIRE

Baddesley Clinton
Coughton Court
Kenilworth Castle
Lord Leycester Hospital
Stoneleigh Abbey
Warwick Castle

WILTSHIRE

Avebury Manor
Glastonbury Abbey
Heale Gardens
Iford Manor
Old Wardour Castle
Pyt House

Salisbury – Malmsbury House

NORTH YORKSHIRE

Flamborough Head – numerous caves
Fountains Abbey
Pickering Castle
Ravenscar – smuggler's signalling post
Ripley Castle
Saltburn – Ship Inn
Scarborough – Three Mariners Inn
Scarborough Castle
Staithes – Cod and Lobster
Welton – Green Dragon Inn
Whitby – Saltergate Inn
    – Ship Launch Inn
    – White Horse Inn

WEST YORKSHIRE

Oakwell Hall
Sandal – Three Houses Inn

WALES

CLWYD

Plas Teg

DYFED

Carreg Cennen Castle

GWENT

Penhow Castle
Raglan Castle
Tredegar House
Treowen Court

GWYNEDD

Caernarvon Castle
Holyhead – disguised pillboxes
Plas Mawr
Snowdonia National Park – Carnedd Dafydd

SCOTLAND

DUMFRIES AND GALLOWAY

Benane Head
Fenwick
Loudoun
Wigtown – Martyrs' Memorials

FIFE

St Andrews Castle

GRAMPIAN

Craigievar Castle
Fyvie Castle
Kildrummy Castle

HIGHLAND

The extensive journey of Bonnie Prince Charlie, by boat,
on foot and on horseback, carried him through too many
places in this region for all of them to be listed here.
Besides, many are far from the beaten track. Better-known
sites connected with the prince's flight include:

Achnangart
Arisaig
Ben Alder
Culloden battlefield
Glen Moriston
Glen Shiel

Isle of Benbecula
Isle of Scalpay
Isle of Skye – Prince Charlie's Point
Isle of South Uist – Prince's Cave
    – Ormaclett
Loch Arkaig
Loch nan Uamh
Loch Nevis

LOTHIAN

Dalkeith Country Park
Stevenson House
Yester Castle

STRATHCLYDE

Elderslie – Wallace Yew

TAYSIDE

Affleck Castle
Castle Menzies
Glamis Castle

Further Reading

As well as the guide books on sale at individual sites, the following books deal in greater depth with some of the topics considered in the text:

Aveling, J.C.H., *The Handle and the Axe: the Catholic Recusants in England*, Blond and Briggs, 1976.

Blount, T., *Boscovel*, Tylston and Briggs, 1894.

Bossy, J., *The English Catholic Community*, Darton, Longman and Todd, 1975.

Campbell, D., *Secret Places*, Banyan, 1989.

Campbell, Duncan, *War Plan UK*, Burnett/Hutchinson, 1982.

Daiches, D., *Charles Edward Stuart*, Thames and Hudson, 1973.

Dashwood, Sir Francis, *The Dashwoods of West Wycombe*, Aurum, 1987.

Deering, C., *History of Nottingham*, Nottingham Civic Society, 1946.

Dobson, R.B. and Taylor, J., *Rymes of Robin Hood: An Introduction to the English Outlaw*, Heinemann, 1976.

Errand, J., *Secret Passages and Hiding Places*, David and Charles, 1974.

Fea, A., *Secret Chambers and Hiding Places*, Methuen, 1901.

Hippisley Coxe, Anthony D., *A Book about Smuggling in the West Country*, Tabb House, 1984.

Historic Houses, Castles and Gardens Open to the Public, British Leisure Publications, 1991.

Hodgetts, Michael, *Secret Hiding Places*, Veritas Book and Video Distribution, 1989.

Hooper, W., *Reigate. Its Story Through the Ages*, 2nd Ed., Kohler and Combes, 1979.

Kenyon, J.P., *The Popish Plot*, Penguin, 1974.

Lampe, David, *The Last Ditch*, Cassell, 1968.

Laurie, Peter, *Beneath the City Streets*, Allen Lane, 1970.

Matthews, William, Ed., *Charles II's Escape from Worcester*, University of California Press, 1966.

Morley, Geoffrey, *Smuggling in Hampshire and Dorset*, Countryside, 1983.

Morris, John, Ed., *Troubles of Our Catholic Forefathers*, 3 vols., reprinted by Gregg International, 1970.

Noall, Cyril, *Smuggling in Cornwall*, D.B. Barton, 1971.

Ollard, Richard, *The Escape of Charles II After the Battle of Worcester*, Constable, 1986.

Pearman, H., *Caves and Tunnels in South-East England*, 1988.

Phillipson, David, *Smuggling: A History 1700–1970*, David and Charles, 1973.

Pringle, Patrick, *Stand and Deliver. The Story of the Highwayman*, Museum Press, 1951.

Ross, Stewart, *Scottish Castles*, Lochar, 1990.

Squiers, Granville, *Secret Hiding-Places*, S. Paul, 1933.

Thompson, H.A., *Military Architecture in England During the Middle Ages*, Clarendon, 1912, reprinted 1975.

Trench, R. and Hillman, E., *London Under London*, Murray, 1985.

Warner, P., *Sieges of the Middle Ages*, Bell, 1960.

Warner, P., *The Medieval Castle*, Bell, 1971.

Waugh, Mary, *Smuggling in Kent and Sussex 1700–1840*, Countryside, 1985.

Wills, Henry, *Pillboxes*, Leo Cooper/Secker and Warburg, 1985.

Wood, George Bernard, *Smugglers' Britain*, Cassell, 1966.

Index

188